W9-ATX-870

Paw Prints in My Soul

Lou Dean

CLINESCOT
PUBLISHING
COLORADO

Paw Prints in My Soul

Copyright © 1997 by Lou Dean Jacobs

ISBN: 1-56865-787-0

Printed in the United States of America

CLINESCOT
PUBLISHING
COLORADO

Blue Mountain Road
Dinosaur, Colorado 81610

Acknowledgments

Thanks

To Robert H. Williams for helping me produce and promote *Angels in Disguise*, and for teaching me the Law of the Universe.

Michael Phillips and Al Hartmann of the *Salt Lake Tribune* for front-page coverage of Jake saving my life in 1993.

CBS This Morning for coming to the ranch and inviting me to tell my story on national television.

People Magazine for the cover story in December 1996 of ordinary people, touched by angels.

To the unknown Ojibwa for his prayer.

Mary Peace Finley, who lifted and pushed me forward when my passion to write became smothered beneath rejection slips.

To Allen for taking good care of my animals while I promoted my first book and to Gerry for helping me keep my sense of humor through it all.

My dogs, Doubleday, Angel, and Sissy. To Marvin, my twelve-toed cat. My horses, Cocoa, McKay, Percolate, Cassey, and Heck. All of you gave me lots of nurturing love while I wrote this book. Special thanks to my jackass, Jesse James, for waking me up every morning at five and starting my day with a kiss.

Dedicated to

SHORTY

I still love you with my whole heart.
During the difficult times,
your paw prints were alone on the creek bank.

Grandfather,
Look at our brokenness

We know that in all creation
Only the human family
Has strayed from the Sacred Way.

We know that we are the ones
Who are divided
And we are the ones
Who must come back together
To walk in the Sacred Way.

Grandfather,
Sacred One,
Teach us love, compassion, and honor
That we may heal the earth
And heal each other.

OJIBWA PRAYER

I

"The itsy bitsy spider went up the water sprout. Down came the rain and washed the spider out. Out came his wings and the spider flew to Fob, and now he likes to sing and sit upon the log."

Pat Dog followed my tiny fingers up and around, then tilted her head as I fluttered them to the grass. She smiled at me and asked me to tell her more.

Holding a worn copy of a Sears Catalog, upside down, I began again. "Fob is a wonder. He has fox fur and face, with bird wings and feathers. Sometimes he visits me in my dreams and I fly with him to the white beach where the rainbow touches the sea."

Pat Dog's jaws snapped and she caught the pesky fly that'd been swarming us. She worked the dreadful creature to the end of her tongue and let him drop in a dribble lump. The motion caused the bonnet I'd placed on her head to fall under her chin next to Mama's blue beads.

"You must not kill flies while I teach, honey. It makes me lose my place." Pat Dog's head dropped onto her paws and she looked at me with apology in her deep eyes. I straightened the bonnet.

I looked at the plastic watch on my wrist. Its pretend time was stuck forever in one position, which didn't matter. I couldn't tell time anyway. "It's your turn for the gum, dear." I took the wad of bubble gum from my mouth and offered it. She licked it from my fingers and began to chew, diligent to keep the wad from sticking to her long teeth.

"Mama's told you about lettin that dog chew your gum." The front screen door slammed with a bang behind me as Sis and Bub clanked out carrying their lunch buckets and books. "She'll get onto you for it," Sis said.

"It'll make you puke," Bub warned, grabbing his throat with one hand and choking until his face turned scarlet.

I raised a shoulder and let it fall in a dramatic shrug like I'd seen my older sister do. "We don't care, do we girl?" Pat Dog lifted her paw for me to shake. "See?"

"You girls try to stay out of trouble today," Sis said, giving my pigtails a playful swat.

"Next year we will be goin up across those terraces with you. Pat Dog can't wait to be in school."

"She told you that, Sissy?" Bub asked, kneeling beside me.

"Yes. Every day when we walk to meet you in the afternoon, we talk about it. She says she can't wait until yesterday."

"Tomorrow." Bub said. "Yesterday's gone, remember? Tomorrow isn't here yet."

"Well, the other yesterday," I snapped, and I frowned until he laughed.

"You two can play in my playhouse today. Just leave my stuff alone and take all of your bottles and junk out when you leave."

"Did you hear that, dear?" I squealed out the exciting news, and Pat Dog jumped to follow me down the path that led to Bub's playhouse.

"Thanks, Bub," I hollered as my brother walked fast toward the red brick schoolhouse in the distance. With the next breath I began making the morning plans. "First we'll go get our little bottles and some food colors from Mama, load the wagon, mix our magic potions. Then we'll come back to our house and cook dinner."

Pat Dog sat, listening to every word, chewing the gum with slow chomps.

"It's my turn now," I said, glancing at my watch. "Besides, I'll have to take it before I go to the house or Mama might notice." I put my hand out, and she obediently opened her mouth and pushed her tongue around until the gum fell into my hand. I popped it back into my mouth and took off with my friend at my heels.

"So you ladies are going to make dinner today?" Mama asked, as she put the tiny bottles of food coloring in a cigar box and handed it to me. "Well, how nice. Maybe I'll join you."

"Could you, Mama?" The idea filled me with delight.

"Why don't you come get me when it's all ready? We'll see. I have all these turnips to can." I looked around at the peelings piled high in the sink and the baskets of dirty turnips fresh from the garden, and I heard lids jittering as puffs of steam burst from a pan on the stove.

"I could help you, Mama."

Mama smiled down at me as she started removing jars from a steaming pot. "It's okay, honey. You and Pat Dog run along and make us some dinner."

"Maybe we'll have lobster and you can bring peanut butter and jelly."

Mama laughed. "So I suppose you need some bacon rind for the crawdads? Excuse me, I mean lobsters."

"Yes, please."

She walked to the icebox, took out a slab of bacon, and cut a thick piece of fat and rind. From the drawer next to the sink, she drew out a ball of heavy twine and cut a long piece.

"See you ladies for dinner."

"Can we wear the dress-up clothes, Pleasssee?"

"The box is in the bottom closet on the porch," Mama said as she began to squeeze chunks of white turnips into hot jars.

I slipped the worn shawl over Pat Dog's shoulders, and it dragged along behind as I wobbled forward in high heels, stumbling the first few steps. I gathered up a wad of my skirt with one hand, lifted my head, and started down the path to the creek.

With the wagon loaded, Pat Dog led the way. My box of colored glass bottles, dishes, and buckets rattled, and the wagon wheels squeaked as we made our way out of the yard, down the hill.

"Now you can dig where I tell you. In no time we'll have our lobsters and be on our way." I walked along the creek until I saw the first telltale mud pile above a crawdad hole. "Here, girl, right here." I pointed, and Pat Dog went to work. Getting her back and shoulders into the job, she dug with a vengeance, flinging soft bits of mud up under her belly and behind her in the air. Soon, a perfectly round hole became visible on the creek bank.

"Good job," I said, slapping my friend gently on the shoulders. "Here it goes." I lowered the bacon rind into the hole and waited. Within minutes I felt a tug and slowly raised my string. A colorful red and green crawfish dangled from the rind with one pincher clinched to the bacon in a stubborn grip.

I lowered our catch into a rusty bucket. "We got him, girl. Now two more. One for you. One for me."

Pat Dog walked along beside me until I pointed to the next mud pile. She immediately went to work.

Pat Dog watched as I prepared dinner. On a stump table in Bub's playhouse, I poured water into bottles and added drops of food coloring until I had a rainbow row of glistening "soda pop."

Using soft mud from the creek bank, I pressed perfect pies and fluted the edges the way Mama had taught me. With a rock, I mashed last year's pecan shells into crunchy bits and pressed them into my crusts.

From my assortment of junk in the wagon, I brought out three chipped plates and bent forks, cleared the table, and placed a frayed flour sack over it with great ceremony. I crowded the plates, forks, and bottles in place. Stepping back, I sighed with deep satisfaction.

"What do you say, Mrs. Paterson?" Pat Dog stood, looked at the table, and wagged her tail. The crawdads were making scratchy sounds as they tried to escape by climbing the walls of the rusty bucket.

"Patience," I said to them, peering down. I used the exact same tone that Mama used when she said the word to me.

"Mrs. Paterson, shall we drive to town now and fetch Mrs. Jacobs?"

From the open window above the kitchen sink I could hear my mother's voice singing "You Are My Sunshine." The sound of her happiness made me smile.

Pat Dog wagged her tail and lifted a paw to me. I invited her to ride in the wagon, and she obediently jumped in. Adjusting her shawl, beads, and bonnet, I kissed her on the nose. "You look especially pretty today, dear."

When we reached the porch steps, I was still chattering. "Do you really think so, Mrs. Paterson? Well, I swear. I'll only be a minute now. You stay in the wagon."

"Dinner is ready, Mrs. Jacobs," I said, walking up behind Mama and tugging at her pants leg.

"Oh honey, I have to get these done so I can start weeding the garden. I have two loads of laundry to do and then supper to start." She turned from the sink, wiped sweat from her forehead, and looked at me.

I pushed my face into an exaggerated pout and dipped my head. "But dinner's all ready, Mrs. Jacobs. We have lobster and pecan pie and strawberry soda pop."

Mama burst out laughing. Her bubbly giggle vibrated from the steamy ceiling, danced happily off the kitchen curtains, and flipped on the breeze back into my ears.

I grinned and rubbed the dirt from the top of one bare foot with the heel of the other.

"Oh, to hell with it," Mama said, dropping the turnip and knife in the sink. She drew out the huge jar of peanut butter and reached for the bread and jelly. With quick swipes, she constructed the sandwiches, then cut them into tiny squares.

"Shall we go, Miss Ludee?"

Pat Dog sat in the wagon, eyes on the door. Her bonnet drooped slightly to one side on her lowered head. When she heard us coming, her tail flopped wildly and she jumped from the wagon. Her shawl caught on the rough wagon edge, and she gasped and choked when it tightened around her neck.

"Mrs. Paterson, patience," I said in an impatient tone.

Mama laughed again, the bubbly glee spilling out into the warm wind. "So tell me, ladies, is the lobster fresh?"

"Oh yes, Mrs. Jacobs. Very fresh. Isn't that right, Mrs. Paterson? Today's catch." Pat Dog wagged her tail and smiled at us.

In the playhouse, I seated my guests and proceeded to serve— one crawfish on each plate, one wedge of pecan pie, and choice of colorful soda pop.

"This is delicious, Miss Ludee," Mama said, taking small nibbles from the peanut-butter sandwich. "What a lovely day for a lobster brunch, Mrs. Paterson."

"What day is it?" I asked, forever curious about all of the wonderful things Mama had to offer.

"A lovely Wednesday in March, 1953."

"And I was born in 1958," I beamed.

"In 1948. Soon you will be this many."

Mama held up all of the fingers on one hand, and I stretched myself taller, a sense of pride bursting through me.

Pat Dog chewed tiny pieces of peanut-butter sandwich, taking quiet bites from her plate and chewing slowly, as she'd been taught. Her crawdad crawled desperately around on the plate in front of her. She watched it as she worked the peanut butter off of the roof of her mouth.

"Brunch," Mama repeated. "B-R-U-N-C-H. Meaning, a late breakfast, an early lunch, or a combination of the two."

"Between breakfast and dinner?" I was getting confused. Lunch wasn't a word that we used on the farm.

"Here in Osage County we call our meals breakfast, dinner, and supper," Mama explained, "but in other parts of the country people have breakfast, lunch, and dinner. They don't say supper."

I pondered on that for a moment. So many interesting things to learn. So many other places besides Oklahoma. So many words I could still discover.

"Ohhhh," Mama squealed when her crawdad managed to jerk himself over the edge of her plate into her lap. She carefully grabbed him by the back, avoiding the pinchers that were thrashing in the air, and placed him in the rusty bucket beside our table. She then did the same with the crawdads on our plates.

"Well, ladies, it's been . . ." She hesitated, and I knew what she was doing — trying to give me another word. Sometimes she'd give me three or four in one day and have me tell them back to her at bedtime. "Fascinating. F-A-S-C-I-N-A-T-I-N-G. Extremely interesting or charming."

"Fascinating." I let the wonderful word roll off of my tongue. "Fascinating. That's like my Fob — that's his word. I know it for sure because he makes me sparkle inside with happy bubbles."

Mama's laughter filled the playhouse, and Pat Dog's tail erupted, sending bottles of colored water splashing. "Your Fob?" Mama asked, helping me clean the mess.

"He visits me at night in my dreams, and we fly away to a beach full of white sand and rainbows and bubbles."

Mama looked at me, smiling, but then the strangest expression crossed her face. Like a cloud passing in front of the sun, her joy disappeared, and it was replaced by something so cold, so sharp, it cut into my heart.

"What is it, Mama?" I asked, touching her hand.

She jerked me up into her arms and squeezed me breathless, then she started out of the playhouse. "I have work to do," she said, and I saw her brush dampness from her face as she disappeared toward the house.

Pat Dog and I cleaned Bub's playhouse spotless so that he'd be sure and let us return. We took the crawdads back to the creek.

"Good-bye, Mr. Crawdad. Thanks for playin with us." I lay and watched as they left the prison of the rusty bucket and sauntered happily back toward their mud homes. I wondered what life must be like down beneath the surface of the creek with the fish, snails, and snakes.

"It must be fascinating," I told Pat Dog. "Like my Fob."

Pat Dog lay beneath the cottonwood trees, and I snuggled my head into her thick, chubby side for a pillow. We took a nap and traveled together to a fascinating land of rainbows, bubbles, and brunches.

Two weeks later on a warm April afternoon, I was playing near the creek when I heard a rifle shot ring out from near Dad's shop. I took off running to find Pat Dog. She hated guns and loud noises and would come running to find me anytime Dad started shooting. I felt a twang of guilt because I hadn't spent much time around my friend the last several days. She'd killed a skunk the week before, and, in spite of several baths, she still reeked from the dreadful odor.

To the yard, around the playhouse, out toward the barn I ran, calling her name. I heard Dad hollering and saw Mama come blasting out of the house. Something was wrong. I started toward my dad to see if I could help.

"Stay back, Sissy," he bellowed, motioning me with a broad, angry sweep of his muscular arm.

It was too late. I saw the familiar black figure on the ground, flopping and kicking. I heard another crack of the rifle and realized what Dad was shooting.

"NOOOO!" I screamed, running toward my old dog. Her back feet jerked one last time, then the gray haze over her eyes stared cold. I shrieked out to her, wanting her to know that I was near. I struggled forward, but Dad's strong arm pulled me back. I turned on him, biting and kicking and squalling.

"She was sick, Sissy, slobbering and having a fit. I'm sorry — I had no choice." His words tunneled somewhere way back in my mind and made my anger turn to icy reality. I turned from him and stared in horror at my friend. Her beads were twisted up tight around her neck, and the bonnet was under her jaw, oozing with thick blood.

"Get the shovel, Bub," I heard Dad say above the roar of emotions in my ears. "Johnnie, would you get Sissy out of here?"

"For God's sake, Dean, couldn't you wait until I took her somewhere or . . . ."

"I'm sure you could have done it better," my dad snapped, then in a tone of defeat he added, "I killed another rabid skunk this morning. Pat Dog was slobbering."

"I'm pretty damned certain I could have at least made sure that Sissy was in the house." Mama had my hand, holding me away as she argued.

My eyes were glued to the lifeless black body, the fur blowing gently in the warm breeze. I prayed for some sign of movement, for the eyes to blink. I wanted to take her up in my arms one last time, feel her warm fur against my face, tell her she couldn't go. I needed her to play dress up, make pecan pies, and catch crawdads. Share gum with me.

Bub returned, threw the shovel to the ground, and grabbed me up in his arms. He gave me such a squeeze that a giant sob squalled out from the deepest part of my heart, and for a moment I felt cold and sweaty at the same time.

"Come on, Sissy," Bub said, leading me off toward the creek.

That night I had terrible dreams. I was walking near the trees, searching for Pat Dog, for Fob. And something started chasing me. I couldn't see it, but the feeling of its presence sent a chill into my very bones. I awoke screaming. I was sitting straight up in bed howling like some rabbit caught up in a wolf's jaws. Mama carried me into the kitchen, sat me on the counter, and ran hot water from the kitchen sink over my legs, rubbing the pains away.

"What was it, Mama? Why was it chasin me?"

"It's Brutal. B-R-U-T-A-L, the cruel and ruthless fear that visits us in life. When we face him, he begins to turn away."

Every night Brutal chased me in my dreams. I'd awake screaming and Mama would carry me to the kitchen sink and soak my aching legs in soothing warm water. Each night before I went to sleep, Mama told me to search for Fob in my dreams. I tried desperately. When I said my prayers out loud to Mama I asked please for Fob to return to me and help me through the awful nightmares. But my fascinating friend became elusive and wouldn't return for many years.

II

"Shorty stay with me today?" My baby brother's blue eyes were intense as he followed me and my dog to the edge of the yard.

"Shorty can't miss school, Lil Bub."

"PLEASE, Sissy. I hate bein here by my ownself all day."

I did worry about my little brother. Mama had been gone for several months and Dad worked all morning and slept in the afternoon so that he could work nights on his railroad job. I remembered how lonely it used to be when I was little and Sis and Bub left every morning for school — if it hadn't been for my best friend, Pat Dog.

The memory caused my throat to thicken. "Well, I guess Miss Hedberg won't get upset just this once if her little canine boy is absent."

"Shorty, you want to stay home with Lil Bub?" Shorty's tail thumped against my overalled leg, and he looked from me to my little brother.

"Come 'ere, boy," Lil Bub begged.

Shorty took one hesitant step, and Lil Bub snagged him up in a death grip. My dog gave me a mixed look of compassion and regret, but he licked my little brother's face.

"Shorty says, okay, but just this once." I knelt and rubbed my terrier behind the ears. "I'll explain to teacher. See you this afternoon, Buddy."

"Tell me the story, Sissy."

"What story, Lil Bub?"

"When Shorty said he was yours that first day he was born."

I rubbed my brother's carrot-top head and grinned. "You'll have your own dog someday. A dog is gonna find you somehow and tell you that he's yours."

"Really, Sissy? Dad will let me keep him?"

His last question made me wince. I thought about the long struggle I had with my father before he allowed Shorty to stay.

"Sure he will. You wait and see." I tried to make the words bounce out with enthusiasm, but they stumbled along the way.

Sis and Bub came banging out the screen door, scuffling over a tablet. They continued swatting at one another as they passed me.

"See ya, Lil Bub," my older brother said as he walked by.

"Later, Bubby," Sis said, giving Lil Bub a pat.

Thunder rolled softly as the three of us trailed up across the terraces toward the school building at the crest of the hill.

"It's gonna rain like a cow pissin on a flat rock," Bub said, kicking clods in front of him as he walked. "Need it — a good, steady rain on the wheat."

"You and your redneck expressions," Sis said.

Bub walked up behind Sis, lifted her hair, and stared at her neck. "There's red on your neck, too, sister dear."

I ignored the bickering and put my mind on the troubling phone conversation I'd overheard that morning between Mama and Dad. "Okay, Johnnie," Dad said, "if divorce is what you want." Then he'd slammed the phone down and started banging pots around making breakfast.

Mama hadn't been back to the farm for months, but she had visited us twice, and she was calling often. Once when I was only six, she left, then returned after a few months. It never occurred to me that she wouldn't return this time. But something about the tone of Dad's voice that morning had a hint of finality.

And that word — "divorce." I stretched my mind to recall where I'd heard it before. I quickened my steps, anxious to get to Miss Hedberg's desk and the fat dictionary.

When we reached the fence, Bub stomped the two bottom wires and pulled the top two high so that Sis and I could get through. My brother then put his right thumb to his nostril, snorted, and let a stream go shooting toward the ground. It zipped out on the rising wind, hung from Bub's elbow, and connected to the fence post.

"Dad can do it every time," Bub mumbled with a puzzled frown.

"That's disgusting," Sis said, turning away as she gathered her skirt with its swishing can-can petticoat. "And," she said, straightening herself on the other side, "just so you know — I'm no redneck. Just because I was born in this godforsaken place doesn't mean I have to stay here." Then when Bub didn't try to argue, Sis added, "I'm going off to Hollywood one day and marry Elvis."

Bub let out his fine rolling laugh. It echoed out over the damp hills and bounced happily into my ears until I grinned. "Why would the king of rock and roll want to marry a redneck girl from Osage County, Oklahoma?"

Sis stuck out her tongue, then stomped on ahead.

"Well, I'm gonna join the Air Force." My brother got a faraway look in his steel blue eyes and paused for a deep breath of stormy air. "Be a fighter pilot. Froooomm," he said, turning in the field and looking toward the sky. After a minute he said, "What about you, Sissy Gal? What's your dream?"

"I'm stayin right here on this farm forever. Me and Shorty and my animals." I blurted the words, fiercely impatient to get to school and to the dictionary.

Sis cackled out a hateful chuckle. "Little dreams for little girls," she said. "Almost nine years old and all she wants to do is stay with Mama and Daddy forever and ever."

I leveled a squinted stare at my sister's back. Since she'd become a teenager, she thought she was Miss Priss. "Shut up," I snapped.

"Make me, you little backward tomboy. Still running around the creek with your shirt off, painting yourself with pokeberry juice and pretending you're a wild Indian. Even Peter Pan had to grow up."

The screen door slammed below and we all turned. Lil Bub's speck moved slowly across the yard and blurred beneath the elm trees. I could see him in my mind, his hands jammed down into overall pockets, red-orange hair in tight knots, and his bottom lip in a pout. I was thankful I'd left Shorty with him.

"One of these years," I said, drawing in a breath, before you know it, Lil Bub will be comin up over these terraces with us."

"I'm sure school will be a relief from being around Dad all day. He's such a prince of good moods lately," Sis said. "I know why, too." Sis turned and looked directly at me. "Mama's got a boyfriend."

I stopped dead still and stared at Sis's back. "What?" I asked. The word squeaked out of my mouth like a tree-frog chirp.

Sis turned, slapped her hand on her hip, and smirked. "And she wants a divorce, too."

"Why don't you shut up," Bub said.

Sis's words sent a shudder through me, like a dog shaking the life out of a rat. "Take it back," I said, first in a bare whisper, then louder. "Mama can't have a boyfriend. What about Dad?"

Sis stopped again and turned. "You know what you are? A bowlegged, kinky-haired, flat-chested little *girl.*"

I reached down into the soft plowed field and grabbed a dirt clod. "Take it back," I choked, walking fast to narrow the distance between us. "Miss know-it-all!" I screamed

Sis dropped to one knee and put both hands over her heart. "Your words — they pierce my tender heart," she said in her actress voice.

"You have the heart of a sand wasp," I yelled, then drew back and fired the clod up across the field. The bullet found its mark, thudding her with a soft spray of red dirt.

Sis stood in shock for an instant, then bent to grab a clod. Bub immediately peppered her with several stinging blaps that made her dance in a frustrated circle.

I kept tossing as fast as I could, screaming, "Take it back!"

"Stop it!" Sis finally screamed, jumping up and down in a fit and covering her face with her hands. "Stop it, you little brats. You've ruined me." Her white blouse that had been stiffly starched drooped from her shoulders, limp and dust speckled. Her fluffy ponytail hung off to one side, dirty and damp. Before she had a chance to straighten herself, the hum of the high-school bus came whining across the calm.

"Ooooohhhh!" Sis squealed, dusting her clothes. Then she scurried up over the last terrace as the yellow bus inched its way to a stop on the country road.

A slow rain began to sprinkle over me. In the far distance came the sound of a hand bell from the steps of Braden School. I snatched up my Big Chief tablet, books, and lunch pail and rattled off behind Bub.

"Bub," I said, grabbing his overalls leg loop when he started up the school steps. "Sis doesn't know what she's sayin, does she? How could Mama like someone besides Dad? What's divorce mean, anyway?"

Bub stopped, reached, and wiped red dust from my nose. "You've got dirt on your freckles, Sissy." A half-grin slid across his face, then he shifted his weight from one foot to the other. A blast of wind slammed against the door, bringing sheets of pouring rain. Bub pushed me inside and closed the door behind us.

That afternoon when Miss Hedberg rang the hand bell after last hour, I stumbled toward home like a colt new to the saddle. The word I learned that morning sparked a terror in my chest so intense I could still barely breathe.

D-I-V-O-R-C-E '"To end marriage . . .to terminate . . .to dissolve." It was Mama who'd taught me about words and how important definitions were. As I stumbled across the school yard that afternoon, I hated her and the new word that she'd given me that day. I thought about what fun Mama and I used to have in Bub's play-house with our pretend brunches — my sharing with her how fantastic Fob was. Anger churned inside me, burning like the sting of a red ant. How could she divorce us?

I could hear my little brother's shrill voice before I crossed the gravel road and started through the field.

"Sissy, come quick."

Afraid that something was wrong with Shorty, I took off in a dead run. "What, Lil Bub? What's wrong?" I asked, kneeling to check my dog.

"I've seen him, only he's a she and she's the grandest. This mornin I went to play . . . I heard this noise. Shorty saw her first and. . . ."

"Whoooa," I said. "Slow down. Who is she?"

"A dog — my dog. She wouldn't come to me, but she let me closer. I snuck her part of my dinner. Shorty went up, and they sniffed. He walked around all stiff-legged with his tail straight in the air just whippin." My little brother stopped and sucked in a quick breath. "Sissy, she told me."

"Told you?"

"She's gonna be my dog. I know it, Sissy."

I looked at his pale face, the dark freckles scattered across his nose like apple seeds on snow. A tug of fear pulled at my belly. "Not so fast, Lil Bub. She could belong to someone or be sick or . . . who knows. Don't go gettin your hopes all up."

"Come on, hurry." He grabbed me and started off.

"You haven't told Dad?"

"I ain't stupid," he said with a disgusted sigh.

I followed my little brother into the waist-deep weeds behind the barn near the grapevines that hung from the giant cottonwoods on the creek. His voice squeaked out in a call.

"Here, pretty gal, come on. It's okay."

We stood watching for movement. Shorty's eyes were alert and his ears perked.

The first glimpse of the sharp nose and keen eyes that appeared in the brush made me jump. "Lil Bub, it's a coyote," I said, grabbing his shoulder to hold him back.

The sparkling eyes staring at us were wolflike, wild and alert. The coat was a thick and glossy tan with a golden sheen like a wolf's. She didn't look like any dog I'd ever seen.

"Ain't she grand?" My little brother had a death grip on the leg loop of my overalls, and his fingers were trembling.

Shorty bounced out of the brush into the clearing, and the stranger's sharp eyes disappeared.

"Darn you, Shorty," Lil Bub said as he started crashing out from our hiding place.

In the next instant, the dog was in the clearing, wagging a shaggy tail at her new friend. Shorty greeted her with his tail flipping wildly, and they began smelling each other. I could see then that she wasn't pure coyote. Her body was too thick and her features were different, but her color and movement denoted some part wild dog.

A terror born of reality streaked through me. If she had been living wild, it meant that she'd kill most anything for food — chickens, ducks, piglets, lambs. Dad would shoot her on the spot if she made one move toward the stock.

I lived in fear the next few weeks, and my nights were haunted by Brutal. The word "divorce" kept echoing through my dreams, and I saw my mother with a faceless stranger. My little brother often joined me in my haunting nightmares. Brutal would be carrying Lil Bub's dog off, and I'd be running as fast as I could while my brother called my name. "Sissy, help me, Sissy."

I'd awake in a tangle of damp sheets, my legs aching, and I'd walk to the bathroom. In the shower, I'd let my tears disappear beneath the warmth of water while I rubbed my aching legs.

After the dreadful dreams, going back to sleep was hopeless. Instead I'd sneak out my bedroom window, and Shorty and I would walk along the creek until first light. I'd discuss my worries with my friend.

"Lil Bub needs that dog, especially with Mama gone and Dad workin most of the time. And lately Dad is a mess — home brew on his breath all the time and his clothes sweaty from working in the field. He shouts out orders and growls chores. How can we reason with him about the dog?"

Shorty would follow patiently, sometimes giving his little "Errf" of agreement, other times talking to me with his eyes.

"You're right, buddy. I can't worry about all this at once."

My little brother named his new friend Shadow. It took the better part of a week before she let him pet her, and even then, she always returned to the shelter of the brush. By some miracle, Dad hadn't caught sight of her.

Each morning when I left for school, Lil Bub would be sitting on the porch, waiting for his chance to escape to see Shadow. Every afternoon he met me at the top of the terraces jabbering about "his dog."

I helped him steal scraps for Shadow, although I was fairly certain that she could take care of herself. My main concern was hiding it all from Dad no matter what the cost. If I had to lie, cheat, or steal, I didn't care. I'd never seen Lil Bub so happy. He needed Shadow, and I would pay for the consequences when they arrived.

One Saturday morning Mama called and Dad screamed at her over the phone the whole time we ate our oatmeal. "You can take them for the day," he finally said. "But if *he's* with you, don't pull onto my property. I mean it. You stop at the cattle guard. I'll send the kids up."

Dad came back to the table with a steaming cup of coffee and stared blankly at his cold oatmeal for several minutes before he spoke. "Your . . . mother . . ." He said the word like a curse, then seemed to choke. "Your mother is coming to pick you up tomorrow at noon. You can walk to the cattle guard to meet her. She's — well, she has a boyfriend who's coming with her. And I guess she's filing for a divorce."

His words lodged in my throat like a chunk of apple. I wanted to ask him how Mama could do such a thing. I still had a hundred questions about divorce, but the dead look in his eyes stopped me. His face was crusty with dust from plowing all night, and his usually clean-shaven face prickled with stiff red hair.

"Get started on your chores," he barked, and we all bounced in different directions. It was housecleaning day for Sis and me, which included the mountain of laundry and ironing. Bub had barn chores, and Lil Bub, who usually followed Dad, instead clung to my side most of the morning.

"What's Dad mean, Sissy? How can Mama have a boyfriend? Will she bring her new friend to live with us on the farm? What's divorce, anyway? Is she coming home soon?"

"Go away!" I finally screamed. When my younger brother ducked his head and went out the door, I cursed. I worked in a frenzy the next hour in a futile attempt to erase the guilt and his haunting questions.

I was pulling heavy, wet overalls from the washer when Bub came blasting into the house. He went to the gun rack that hung against the east wall on the porch and yanked the shotgun from its peg. Without saying a word, he blasted back out, letting the door bang.

For a moment, I continued what I was doing. Standing on the step stool, I dragged the last of the wet overalls out and dropped them in the basket. I flopped the clothespins on top and started out the door to the clothesline. Bub fetched the shotgun to Dad for many reasons. It was late spring, and snakes appeared on the farm like limbs after a rainstorm. Sometimes on any given day, Dad would shoot three or four poisonous snakes near the creek or the pump house.

Before I got halfway across the yard, I heard Lil Bub's shrill voice.

"Noooo. . . ." It was a terrified, begging plea.

Cold fear sliced through me. I stood perfectly still, my mind frozen. It was like I'd just seen a twister cloud on the horizon dropping down from a dark sky. The feeling of knowing that I had to run, but being slightly suspended in my fear.

When reality returned, I dropped the clothes basket with a thump and made a mad dash around the corner of the house toward the creek.

Dad was pushing fat shells into the double-barrel shotgun and bellowing at Lil Bub. "Stand back, Lil Bub. Do it now."

Beyond my little brother, across the creek, Shadow stood with her head and shoulders camouflaged in the brush.

"Dad, she's mine," Lil Bub squalled, tears rushing as my father drew up his gun.

The memory of Dad shooting Pat Dog returned — the shots banging in my ears, that first reality when I stood above my best friend, staring in horror at the lump of bloody black fur. Lil Bub couldn't stand it.

Vaulting over the fence with bare toes and both hands, I scampered toward my brother, who started wading across the creek toward Shadow.

"Dad, you can't do it. She's my dog...." Lil Bub's sobbing rattled above the singing birds.

"Lil Bub, if you don't get out of the way, I swear, I'll switch you good," Dad yelled, trying to step to one side and get Shadow in his sights.

Then, a sudden commotion came out of the wet grass just as Lil Bub climbed the opposite creek bank. A huge water moccasin slithered its ugly head up, not twelve inches from my little brother's face. It coiled and drew back to strike, yellow jaws open wide.

Lil Bub was between Dad's gun and the snake. No one had time to get to him. Everything stopped — Lil Bub's sobbing, Dad's squalling. Even the birds seemed paralyzed, because a deadly silence hung in the heavy sweetness of the spring afternoon.

"My God," Dad said, breaking the quiet with his raspy choke.

With the speed of a wolf, Shadow appeared. She pounced on the threatening snake without fear. Grabbing it toward the tail, she snapped it like cracking a whip. Then with the precision of an athlete confident of his skill, she continued. Backing in a wide circle, popping and flinging the water moccasin, she crunched the snake in her jaws. It was a beautiful display of speed, agility, and passion. When she finally dropped the snake, it made one last twitch, and Shadow reacted with another full tirade until the moccasin lay dead, its creamy belly shining in the afternoon sun.

Lil Bub dived toward Shadow, putting both arms around her neck. The dog's tail flopped shyly, and she dipped her head into the hug like a child unfamiliar with such attention.

Dad lowered his shotgun and took in a deep, ragged breath. His dark-circled eyes stared for a moment in disbelief. "She stays," he said. Then, handing the gun to Bub, he walked back toward the tractor.

"Did you hear that?" Lil Bub screamed, his squeaky voice vibrating on the wind. "She's mine." He took an arm hold around Shadow's neck, sat down, and pulled the shaggy dog into his lap.

"We heard," Bub said. He walked toward Shadow, and the dog shyly sniffed my older brother's hand, then allowed him to touch her head. Bub knelt down and stared first at the dead snake, then at Shadow. "She really is somthan, Lil Bub."

"She's a snake killer, ain't she, Sissy?"

I was still in shock from the entire scene. Emotions flickered across my mind like butterflies around sweet blossoms — fear, grief, disbelief, relief, and joy.

"Sissssyy. Did you hear? She's mine — just like you said. You told me I'd find a dog someday and Dad would let me keep her."

I gave a short laugh. My brother made all the sneaking and worry and sleepless nights sound so simple.

Shorty approached the dead snake, walking stiff-legged around it but keeping a safe distance. Lil Bub giggled and fell backward. I grabbed his wet breech leg and hauled him into the creek. Shadow and Shorty bounced into the water with us, and we splashed and played until Lil Bub and I ran shriveled and shivering toward the house.

That night, for the first time since Pat Dog's death, I caught a fleeting glimpse of Fob in my dreams. At first I didn't recognize him. When I realized it was my Fob, I was blissful and eager to play with him. But when I ran to embrace him, he faded from sight. The more I pursued him, the more elusive he became until he was no longer visible. But I could still feel his comforting presence.

I howled out in despair, asking him why he wouldn't come to me and telling him that I yearned for our old times together — the days of white sand, rainbows, and bubbles. The moment I spoke the words, Pat Dog was with me again. We were in our dress-up clothes, catching crawdads and mixing colored water in pretty bottles. The afternoon sun sparkled through the trees, glistening on our colored water, shining in our eyes.

I awoke laughing and snuggled deep into my covers. Shorty, who slept just below my bedroom window, whined and scratched the side of the house. I slipped into my overalls and out the window.

My dog and I made our way through the moonlight to the creek where Shadow had saved Lil Bub from the snake. My brother's dog appeared across the creek, her coat silvery in the moon. Shorty's tail immediately went up over his back, and he started toward his new friend.

The moon sparkling on the creek brought back the wonder of my dream. I sat and drew my knees up under my chin and replayed the dream in my mind. Fob hadn't left me. He lingered somewhere just beyond reach. In a strange way, I knew that he had something to do with all the good things that happened — my love for Pat Dog, Shorty becoming mine when I needed him desperately, and Shadow killing the snake and saving herself from Dad's shotgun blast.

My soul ached. I marked my cheeks and arms with mud and stripped off my shirt. My growing infatuation with Indians brought me closer to a sense of who I was in the deepest part of my ownself. The farm, my animals, and a passion to be free cried out.

Scuffing one bare foot in front of the other, I began to dance and let my voice groan out strange sounds that erupted from the deepest part of me. I ask the spirits to bring me closer to the mystery of my life, and I thanked Fob for my animals.

The next morning, I awoke on the creek bank with dried mud pulling at my face and my bare toes half-frozen with dew. I sat up and pushed Shorty from my neck.

"Get inside, little girl," Sis was saying, digging the toe of her shoe into my side. "It's time to go meet Mama. You have to clean up."

Her words filled me with dread. Because of everything that had happened with Shadow the day before, I'd completely forgotten about Mama's visit.

Halfway up the gravel road that morning, I decided that Shorty and I would just take off and hide. I was mad at Mama. How could she have some boyfriend?

"You aren't hiding, little girl," Sis said, giving me a shove when I started to exit nonchalantly behind the splintered granary.

When the car appeared at the cattle guard, I stopped and stared. "I don't like him," I said.

Bub let out a husky laugh that rolled out over the field. "You must have real good eyesight, Sissy. I can't even see him yet."

"Well," I said in a huff, "I don't like him. Neither does Shorty." My dog thumped his tail against my leg in agreement. Then, in an attempt to have some control over the situation, I blurted, "Shorty and I are gonna stop this divorce."

Sis laughed and my face flushed. I couldn't believe I'd said such a thing. But as we continued walking, the thought turned into a strange idea and burned me with a savage desire. Maybe we *could* do something. Maybe there was some way to get Mama home and keep her happy. Dad was always saying, "You don't know unless you try."

To my great surprise, it wasn't a man with Mama, but some lady friend. After quick introductions, Mama got out of the car with her suitcases and the woman pulled away.

"Plans have changed," Mama said and gave a nervous laugh. "I'm spending the day here with you all, on the farm."

Dad was hammering away in the shop when we all walked up. His welding hood was propped back on his head, and sweat dripped down in a river from his forehead to his neck and puddled in front of his shirt.

When he looked up and saw Mama, his face contorted with anger. "Damn it, Johnnie, I thought I told you. . . ." He jerked off his hood and flung it toward his workbench. It hit the metal table and bounced, then landed in a spinning circle among metal shavings and pipe pieces.

"Things have changed. I'm alone. Can we talk?"

When they went off into the house, Dad instructed us to sit and start shelling peas. As I fumbled with the pods, my earlier thoughts began to circle in my mind like bees around honey.

"We can stop this divorce." The words again shocked me, but the declaration gave me a great sense of power and filled me with determination.

Before Sis or Bub could respond, Mama and Dad emerged from the house. "Your mother's staying home," Dad said. His voice didn't hold great enthusiasm, but his eyes seemed softer.

The words bounced around in my head like strawberry soda pop tickling into my tummy. I looked down into Shorty's deep eyes and winked. It was a chance. All we had to do was take advantage of the opportunity.

III

Shorty lifted his head with great ceremony as I painted a line down his face with pokeberry juice. He sat very still and seemed to honor the moment. Shadow was not such a willing customer. She dodged the bright purple stain three times until Lil Bub held her head. The result was impressive. Instead of one straight line from forehead to nose, she had a series of jagged starts and stops that gave her even more of an Indian look.

I dabbed the paint on my little brother's face, then my own. Crossing my legs, I straightened my back and looked across the creek.

"A Yauchta Shay Moo." I said the words while raising my hands through the smoke of our small fire. "I am seeking. Lead me to my vision." I closed my eyes and pulled the smoke closer and closer.

"I am hungry," Lil Bub chanted.

"Hush. You can't talk — we're on a spirit quest."

"I don't like this game. You can't talk, can't eat. What's the fun in it?"

I let out a long sigh. "Then go on, get lost so I can concentrate."

"My dog goes, too," Lil Bub said. Shadow immediately followed her small master toward the house.

I stared into the smoke and tried to get back into the spirit of my Indian ritual, but it was no use. All I could see was Connie Brown shivering beneath the school steps.

The day before at school, I realized where I'd heard the word "divorce." Linda Kay reminded me that Connie and Billy Brown's folks were divorced. The Brown kids. They came to school winter and summer without shoes, depended on the teacher for lunch, and were always dirty and lice infested. Connie spent all of recess hovering beneath the school steps like a frightened animal, and the kids at Braden nicknamed her Cootie.

After Linda Kay told me, I went beneath the steps to talk to Connie.

"Is it horrible?" I asked. "Your parents being divorced and all?" When I crawled toward her, she scrunched herself into the corner and stared at me with wide eyes, scratching at the scabs that were always peppered on her arms.

I spent all of my recess time under the school steps that day, but Connie Brown wouldn't utter one word of help. The experience caused a shudder in my shoulders that returned anytime my thoughts settled on divorce. That afternoon when I left for home, I made a solemn vow to myself. Sis and Bub and Lil Bub and I would never end up like the Brown kids. That thought plunged me into my plan to somehow stop Mama from leaving the farm again.

Since reading had always been my source of security, the very next day at school, I headed straight for the bookshelves that made up our small library.

"Errf," Shorty said, bringing me back to the present with a jerk. My dog was looking at me expectantly.

"Okay, okay," I said, standing and kicking out the leaf fire. "It's no use. We might as well go back to our books."

When I carried the stack of books out to my favorite cool spot beneath the willow tree, I smiled to myself. When my teacher asked me why I wanted everything I could find on marriage, I told her, "I'm gonna write a book." The idea so pleased me that I dived into the pages of the first thick volume, scribbling notes in my tablet and feeling smug and quite sophisticated.

The slender branches of the willow tree brushed down in the warm wind and tickled my shoulders as I read. After an hour, I began to have a terrible time keeping my mind on my business. Bub and Lil Bub were scouting the fields nearby for turtles to race in the last day of school terrapin competition. I could hear them talking and laughing in the distance. Sis was riding her Palomino mare, Maybelle, up to meet her friend OraLee. It was such a grand day in late spring, I yearned to play among the butterflies that swarmed the alfalfa blossoms in the hayfield.

But each time I'd get discouraged, I'd force myself to think of Cootie Brown, shivering beneath the school steps.

"All this stuff about love and commitment is more complicated than decimals," I told my dog.

Shorty lifted his head from my lap and looked at me in full agreement, letting his tail thump against the book.

"We have to do it," I told him. Sis just keeps sayin that a divorce will happen, Mama won't stay home for long. Bub says it isn't my problem and I can't change it. Lil Bub, well, I don't want to worry him with it."

Shorty snapped his teeth at a stubborn fly, then agreed with an "Errf."

The day before the school picnic, I felt all prepared to begin the next phase of my plan. I decided to talk to my parents. I'd feel them out and maybe get valuable information that could help me know what I could do to stop the divorce.

Late that afternoon, I knew Dad was plowing in the far pasture. Shorty and I decided a cool jar of iced tea would put him in a talking mood. We jingled up across the field, feet plodding in the soft dust of the path. Shorty cut through the thicket because he knew I loved the lush growth of new grass near the dark places of shade.

The wind popping through the trees reminded me of a circus that we'd gone to once in Ponca City. I thought of the sound that the huge tent made as it slap-

slapped in the wind. Lumpy clouds sifted overhead, flicking me with shadows, and I looked up and giggled. "Look, Shorty — chubby clowns and flyin elephants dancin across the sky."

When I heard the tractor in the distance, I held tight to my jar and bolted out into the clearing. I tried to flag Dad down, but his eyes were first on the ground in front, then on the plow behind.

Plopping down into the soft field, I set the mason jar on a natural shelf of dirt where the plow had sliced. I dug my toes into the black earth and reached two handfuls to hold inside my fists. Shorty scrunched up under my arm.

"We're gonna be farmers, just like Dad," I told my buddy. "We'll go to Oklahoma State and graduate in agriculture, just like him."

Shorty licked my chin and showed his excitement over the idea.

Dad spotted me waving on the edge of the field as he came back around. When he pulled the tractor to a stop, Shorty and I trotted over and Dad gave me a hand up.

"Can Shorty go?"

"If you hang on to him."

I straddled the radiator and felt the heat against my legs. When Shorty felt the warm hum beneath his feet, he dived to the ground and barked his disapproval.

"Okay, then. Wait for me by the fence." I pointed.

My dog took two slow steps, dragging each foot dejectedly as he made his way toward the edge of the field in slow motion.

Dad took long, greedy pulls from the mason jar of tea and then wiped his lips, leaving a clean path across his dirty face. His red, crew-cut stubble was covered by a sweat-stained cap, and the tops of his ears were pink and peeling from too many hours beneath the sun.

"That really hits the spot, P Jink," he said. "How is it you always seem to know when I'm thirsty?"

I warmed at the sound of the nickname Dad had given me. I remembered asking him one day why he called me that. "Because you're a P Jink," he said, grinning.

"Were you real, real thirsty?" I asked.

"I was spitting cotton."

I giggled. It was a game we played. I knew he would say the words, same as I knew there was a water can sitting in the shade at the edge of the field.

"Want to ride a round?" he asked, standing and reaching back to adjust the lever that dropped and lifted the plow.

I agreed with a quick nod, and the tractor jerked forward. I felt scared at first, like always. There wasn't much to hold onto. I clutched the warm hood with my knees and held to it with my hands. I was careful to guard my expression. If I showed fear, Dad would tease me. I was riding backward, facing Dad and watching the plow bite into the stubble field and turn great chunks of earth as easy as a churn against soft butter.

When Dad stopped the tractor with a jerk, I fell forward onto the steering wheel. He pointed in front of the tractor toward the ground. A brown, wing-striped killdeer was putting on a show. The bird was repeating "dee-de-de" and dragging a wing across the ground, limping.

My heart slowed to a thud. "Is she hurt?"

"No," Dad said, "she has a nest out there some- where. She's trying to keep us away."

"We won't run over her home, will we?"

Dad gave his short, impatient laugh, the one that made me feel dumb. When I frowned and looked around at the bird, he said, "It's empty anyway."

Somehow I didn't believe him, and when the tractor jerked forward and the plow turned the earth, I closed my eyes and cringed, and the sound of the bird's cry kept echoing in my mind even after we'd circled the field and stopped on the far side.

When Dad helped me off the tractor, he looked around at the sky. "It's clabbering up, P Jink. We could sure use some moisture, but I hope it holds up a while longer. He hesitated, took out his tobacco and papers, and slowly rolled a cigarette.

The moment was right, but I wondered how to approach my subject. One book stated clearly that reli- gion was important in marriage. "Those who pray together stay together."

I remembered a few years back when we all cleaned up on Sunday and rode the miles into Ponca City to church. I don't know exactly when we stopped or why, but I decided that it might just be a major piece to the puzzle. Also, Grandma Carrie, Dad's mother, was a Christian who never missed a church service.

I watched as Dad finished rolling his cigarette and stuck it into his lips.

"Dad, do you ever miss goin to church?" I asked, climbing down from the tractor.

"Oh, I don't know. Do you?"

I was relieved to see that he was still in a good mood. He talked a good deal more when his spirits were high. "Yes," I said, trying to put a tone of authority into my voice. "I really do. I miss cuttin and pastin the colored pictures, the cookies and punch. . . ."

Dad's husky laughter boomed out over the terraces and I looked up and smiled, wondering what had struck him funny.

"That's about all I got from Sunday school," he said.

I was sorry for my answer. I hadn't meant it that way. Now I'd botched things up. I had to try again. "Don't you think it might help us all — I mean as a family — if we all started goin again?" Then, in an attempt to drive my point home, I added, "Don't you think Grandma Carrie would want us to?"

When Dad's face blackened and he thumped his cigarette out into the field, I knew I'd said too much.

"P Jink, what in hell's name has come over you?" Dad bellowed. "You spend all your time buried in those books and now you're asking me strange questions."

I dipped my head and dug my bare toes into the cool earth. I wanted in the worst way to blurt out my fears — ask him about the divorce and if Mama was thinking about leaving the farm again. Let him know that I wasn't ending up like Cootie Brown, shivering beneath the school steps. But while I stood, trying to choke out the words, he began again.

"I reckon you don't have enough to do," he said. "You run along home and help your Mama with the food for the picnic tomorrow."

"Yes, sir."

Shorty barked a welcome when he saw me coming across the fence. His face was covered with red dirt where he'd been digging after mice.

I stomped toward home with my dusty mason jar. "I did it all wrong, buddy. Understanding grown-ups is hard enough. Tryin to talk to them is impossible."

My dog took off in front of me, deciding that the conversation was over, then stopped when I began again.

"I have to do better with Mama." I gritted my teeth and took a deep breath. "Somehow, someway, I will figure this out." Shorty gave me his encouraging, "Errf."

In the kitchen, potato salad filled two large bowls and baked beans bubbled on the stove with green onions and bacon strips. I thought of the coming school picnic. The breeze ruffled through the faded kitchen curtains and filled me with the magic promise of summer — fun days on the creek, cold watermelon, home-made ice cream, and night games beneath a full orange moon.

From the hallway I stood in silence and watched Mama. Thoughts of her leaving tore at my resolve. How could I possibly find a way to keep her on the farm?

Anger bubbled up and I felt like yelling out my worst fears, screaming them until she listened. But instead, I settled myself and marched in.

"Mama," I said, plopping down on one of the long kitchen benches. "You know what's gonna make me happy tomorrow?"

"What?" Mama asked, turning to smile.

"Eatin a whole mountain of homemade ice cream at the picnic. Drinkin so much strawberry soda pop that I slosh when I walk. Winnin a shiny silver dollar in the terrapin race."

Mama walked from the sink, drying her hands on a flour sack dish towel. She cut a thick slab of crispy, warm bread at the stove, smeared it with fresh apple butter, and handed it to me.

Joining me on the bench, she lifted her legs up. Letting her shoes drop, she wiggled her toes. "What's going to make me happy tomorrow? Let's see. Visiting all the neighbor ladies, standing in the schoolhouse with the long tables of hot food, and hearing the children's squeals of fun float in on the summer wind."

Mama's words filled me with joy. Our talk was going in the right general direction, so I gave it a gentle nudge.

"What big thing would make you happy? I mean if you could choose anything in the entire world?"

That was a stumper, because Mama stopped and her face twisted with thought. "My own car," she said in a dreamlike tone.

"Why do you want a car?" I asked. My memory flashed to the day when I was six and Mama took the old station wagon and left for California. It was the same day that Miss Hedberg enrolled Shorty in school. Did Mama want a car so she could leave again?

"I don't know, exactly," she said, jerking me out of the past. "Having my own car would be freedom. Sometimes all the work and worry of life just . . . gets to me, you know. Having a car, I could get away — just for an hour or so.

"You wouldn't leave again?" My words came out in a whisper, and I watched my mother's eyes for honesty.

"No. No, Ludee. We'd all leave sometimes, just to get away. Go on fine drives to visit relatives. Maybe take in a picture show in Ponca City."

"You promise you wouldn't leave?" I asked, my dark eyebrows squinting into a serious straight line.

"I promise," Mama said, smiling. In the next breath, though, my mother changed the conversation. "You still running from Brutal at night?"

"Not so much now that Shorty is nearby."

"Does your Fob ever visit you?"

I shook my head, impatient to get back to the main conversation.

Mama slammed the damp towel to her eyes and let out a little sob. I reached out and put apple-butter fingers on her arm.

"What is it, Mama?" I asked, my heart swelling with regret over my questions.

"It's nothing," she said, but the tone of her voice had changed from sunshine to dripping rain. "Sissy Gal, go pick me a mess of green onions from the garden."

"A car," I said out loud as Shorty made his way across the barnyard toward me. The thought that Mama might want the car to leave circled in my thoughts like a hawk winging over a field mouse, but I shot it down. Mama promised me that wasn't true. Besides, out of all my study and efforts in solving the divorce dilemma, it was the only clue I'd come up with. If I kept Mama happy, she would surely get her mind off of divorce.

That night at supper, Lil Bub broke the silence with a sharp question. "Guess what?" he squealed, his mouth crammed with cornbread.

"Chew your food first," Mama said.

My little brother took three gulps from his milk, then blurted, "Shadow and Shorty stuck together this afternoon."

Bub gave a short choke and Sis smothered a giggle.

"Out by the barn," Lil Bub continued. "I tried to pull 'em apart, but they wouldn't budge." After several moments of graphic description, Lil Bub packed his jaws with a giant bite of beans.

"Lovely," Dad said, setting his ice-tea mug down with a thump. "She'll probably have a dozen. Twelve little short-legged snake killers. Just what I need."

IV

It was obvious that my dog had fallen in love. He was completely committed to Shadow and was torn between the two of us. Although he still slept just outside my window and was always there at night if I needed him, during the day he spent most of his time with his new wife.

Together, like two best friends, Shadow and Shorty hunted the fields for rabbits and mice. They romped into the creek and splashed the water, barking with joy, then would plop beneath the shade of the giant cottonwoods and nap.

Shorty would remember at times and bolt away from the love of his life to find me.

"Errf," he would say, running up. His warm eyes were brimming with so much happiness that I couldn't be mad at him. As it turned out, my mind was on other things that spring anyway.

On the last day of school, before the picnic, I was talking to the new girl, Carolyn, who'd just moved to the farm adjacent to ours. The idea of having a friend nearby filled me with thoughts of summer fun. Carolyn and I pumped high in the swings, while a lump of kids pushed and shoved on the playground in a game of red rover.

Always in front of my thoughts was the divorce and what I could do to stop it. Mama said that a car would make her happy. I concentrated on visions of my mother driving us kids around, all of us laughing and having a grand time.

It would take a lot of work — I had no idea how much a car would cost. But I had to go for it. I could begin by picking up pop bottles in the road ditches. Bub and I often did that in the summer to get money for soda pop and comic books. I strained my mind to think of other ways to make cash, but the process put me in a bad mood. Money on the farm wasn't that easy to come by.

Dora ran up just as Carolyn and I jumped from the swings.

"Let's make Cootie dance," she said to me, grabbing a hand of gravel.

"No!" Something that I'd often watched and even taken part in — tossing gravel at Cootie's feet — no longer seemed like sport.

Dora turned to stare. "What's wrong with you?"

"Nothin."

"Okay." Dora smirked. "But it may be your last chance. Mom told me that the ladies from Braden Club reported the Browns to the authority, and the county is coming to take Connie and Billie away."

"Away?" I asked in a squeak.

"Yeah," Dora said, lowering her voice. "Mama says when kids are hungry and alone and such, the county can come in and get them and put them in foster homes."

My mind spun with dreadful visions. "What's a foster home?" I asked, but Dora bolted off to join in a game of crack the whip.

The shudder crept slowly across my shoulders, like a fuzzy caterpillar inching its way down a branch. A foster home must be similar to an orphanage. I'd read about them.

"Lord have mercy," I said out loud, my mind reeling. "What if Mama does leave again? What if Dad falls to drinkin and the county comes and..."

"What are you mumblin about?" Bub asked.

My face burned. I wondered how long he'd been near. My brother had a talent for stumbling along just at the wrong moment.

Bub pulled his hand from behind his back and showed off a bunch of buttercups, daisies, and phlox. "Sissy, you go inside and tell the principal I have a surprise for her. Just as soon as Mrs. B walks out the door, grab her bell from the shelf and hide it in the cloakroom."

I gave my brother an impatient glare. I had other, more important things on my mind than one of Bub's stupid jokes. "No," I told him flatly. "She's not my teacher anymore and I'm not helpin you. Besides, I like Miss Hedberg and I'm not makin her mad."

"Come on, Sissy, please. I'll be goin into high school next year." A slow grin slid across Bub's face and his eyes sparkled. "I just want to do somethan . . . well, somethan Mrs. B can remember me by."

The prospect was tempting. Mrs. B had been a part of Braden School for many years. She taught the first four grades and considered herself "principal," giving her the power to wield the paddle, which she did readily and with malice. I had a few burning memories of my own.

"No," I repeated. "Bub, leave me alone. I'm busy."

"I'll give you anything you want from my army stuff," he bribed.

I thought about Bub's canteen and helmets and play guns. But then I remembered that I'd be working toward the car most of the summer and wouldn't have much time to play. The prize wouldn't be worth the risk.

"No," I repeated.

"Remember that time Mrs. B strapped you for rollin crayons across the floor to Randy — how embarrassed and humiliated you were?"

The thought brought the scene back with vivid clarity and my face burned. "Leave me alone, Bub."

My brother shifted his weight and scratched his thick hair. "What do you want then?"

"A place to hide," I blurted, still thinking of the county and foster homes and all of my fears. When I realized what I'd said, I stared up at Bub. I didn't want him to know about my most private thoughts and feelings. He kept telling me that there was nothing I could do to change the problems between Mama and Dad, it wasn't my business.

Bub was studying my face, trying to understand my thinking. His lips slid into a wide grin. "Sissy, I have a place you can hide where no one in the world could ever find you."

His words made me catch my breath. "A real, real, secret, secret place that no one knows about?"

"I swear, Sissy. No one but me. I'll take you to it if you'll help me hide the bell."

With the fears lingering heavy on my mind, I agreed and found myself sucked into Bub's stupid idea.

Mrs. B was full of herself that day. She loved to put on a show. Anytime parents were around, she had a shining smile and twinkling eyes. The transition from her strict, straight-mouthed face to this "party" person always mesmerized me.

She was in the best of spirits all day, scattering sawdust on the hardwood floors. She allowed us to run and slide and skid across the floor after moving our desks into a lump in one corner. After the shining, all of us took a hand in sweeping, hanging penmanship papers, and polishing the blackboards until the little schoolhouse gleamed in the morning light.

I was horrified that I'd become part of Bub's plan. For starters, I had a healthy respect for Mrs. B's chubby hands and her strap, not to mention the thought of Dad finding out. Anytime Mrs. B told Dad about a grievance, we got a second switching at home and extra chores, regardless of the circumstances. One of Mrs. B's worst fits of temper was like a powder-puff pampering compared to Dad's peach-tree switch.

But I followed Bub's directions to the letter and within moments it was done. I'd snatched the bell from its little shelf near the outside door and hid it behind some boxes in the cloakroom. I went back outside to the swings near the front door so that I could watch the reaction. Bub joined me with a high color and half-grin on his face.

Even though the idea of a good hideout appealed to me, I hated myself for letting Bub talk me into his prank. Most of the time his tricks backfired, and as I pumped up slow in the swings, my eyes glued to the school door, I got an uneasy feeling.

When Mrs. B walked out the door of the schoolhouse, Bub looked up. The principal had a bell-ringing ritual. We all knew it by heart. She always walked to the edge of the top step, looked down at her wide wristwatch, smoothed the dress over her forty-inch waist, then lifted her arm high and rang the polished brass hand bell loud and long until all of us scampered in.

Mrs. B looked so lost and confused when she came out the door, I had to choke back a giggle. Bub smothered his laughter behind his hand. Mrs. B started once to go back inside but quickly turned around. She stood for one moment at the top of the steps, then came barreling down like a bull through a chute.

"Time to come. Recess is . . ." she couldn't decide exactly what to yell, and it was no good anyway. Her voice just died beneath the playground chatter in the gusting wind. Cars and pickups began to dot the gravel roads in the far distance, puttering slowly in from four directions to the picnic. A look of panic stormed the teacher's face. Mrs. B had a very rigid sense of order. She wanted every last one of us in the school sitting at our desks when the parents began arriving.

The principal bounded back inside, then charged out again, running down the steps waving her leather strap. She squalled, a Comanche on a raiding party, attacking kids one bunch at a time, swatting the first one in reach and screeching, "Get in!"

When all of us were finally seated quietly behind our desks, afraid to even breathe, Mrs. B stood at the front of the room puffing. Her tight bun of hair was setting off to the side like a wasp's nest that had been slapped with a stick. Her face was blushed nearly purple, and her eyes were focused on Bub.

"Cute," she said, and the word came out like a curse through her clenched teeth. She reached back to her desk and pulled the flower arrangement, dripping from the vase. "I knew this was too good to be true," she said and slammed the flowers down on Bub's desk, sending yellow pollen jutting across a trail of water. "Where's the bell?"

"I swear, I didn't do it. I was outside the whole recess," Bub said, and when Mrs. B continued toward him, reaching for his ear, he dodged. "Sissy did it."

I felt the words come slamming into my brain. I couldn't believe what I'd heard. I shot one quick, murderous glance toward Bub, then looked at the teacher. All eyes were upon me and I squirmed in my seat. If I had to stand to get strapped, I'd wet my pants for sure. I looked around for Miss Hedberg. My friend was still outside, preparing the school yard for the coming competitions.

Then a boy's voice broke the silence.

"I'm the one who hid it." The words brought a new shock to my mind. I looked across the room into the dragonfly-wing eyes of Bobby and felt a warmth spread through me. Bobby slung his dark hair from his forehead with a toss and squared his shoulders, turning to Mrs. B.

In the next instant, voices drifted in from outside and Mrs. B flew to her desk, straightening her hair and trying to regain her composure as she went to greet the first group of parents at the door.

Bub quickly stuffed the flowers back in the vase and, with a smirk of satisfaction, wiped the top of his desk with his sleeve.

Mrs. B was soon lost in the glow of all of the parents and the excitement of exchanging tender gossip tidbits as the ladies carried in steaming dishes of hot food and crowded the folding tables with their treasures.

I was relieved to escape the immediate danger, but my face burned with fear. I knew that if Mrs. B told Dad about the bell, it would mean big trouble.

When everyone finally gathered inside that afternoon for the Lord's Prayer, I was still uncomfortable. The soft scuffle of feet and the muffle of talk finally quieted. For a moment there was nothing but the gentle sound of wind ruffling the papers on the wall and the mixed aromas of the sweet and spicy food. I'd downed two bottles of strawberry soda pop, so I held my breath in the silence, afraid that a belch might jump out and turn all eyes on me.

When Mrs. B excused us to the playground, I tried to catch up to Bub, but he escaped. I made a silent vow to get him later.

Bobby walked right up to me when I was lining up for the footrace. He grinned and gazed at me from beneath spidery lashes.

"Thanks," I said, feeling the intense eyes drift lazily across me. "For what you did earlier."

"I'd do most anything for you, Sissy Gal," he said.

The lingering eyes threw me into such a confusion, I got all off stride in the footrace and took a hard tumble in the dust.

By late that afternoon, I slumped in defeat on the school steps. The entire day turned out to be a disaster. I lost every single event. Twice the older boys tromped on me. I reached my hand to the burning scrape on my chin. The terrapin I held in my other hand started thrashing about in a wild scramble. A shot of yellow pee dribbled over my hand and down my elbow. I held the turtle out to one side to escape the stream. I turned my anger on him.

"Stupid," I said, looking him right in his orange eyes. "Now you want to run, don't you, now that it's all over. I wish I hadn't caught one fly for you." I tried to think of the meanest thing I could say. "I'm gonna take you home and turn you over on your back and leave you in the hot sun in an ant hill."

Bub came skipping down the steps, carrying empty dishes and whistling a gay tune. When he overheard my hateful threat, he let out a chuckle and I turned sparking eyes on him. The whole lousy day was his fault. He'd started everything off on the wrong track by his stupid idea to hide the bell.

"Bub, I'm gonna kill you and tell God you died," I said with a hiss.

"Did it have a rough day?" Bub asked, adding fuel to the fire as he walked around me and started toward the truck.

I wallowed my tongue around and spit with all of my might, but the small wad fell short and landed inches from Bub's boot.

Bub, looking back, went into a hysterical, hooting squall that ended in song, "Sissy and Bobby sittin in a tree, K-I-S-S-I-N-G."

Angry tears boiled up in my eyes.

"Well, is it gonna cry for me?" Bub teased.

Before I could squelch the urge, I bounded toward him and jumped on his back. Bub fell forward and we were in the dust, dishes broken on the ground in front of us. I pounded, my arms flashing out like windmill blades in a March wind. Bub raised his hands to protect himself from the flogging. He was still laughing, and the sound of it drove me further into a blind rage.

Shorty appeared and yanked viciously on Bub's breech leg. The attack made Bub laugh harder.

Dad jerked me up by the cuff of the neck and grabbed Bub's arm. He half carried, half dragged us to the pickup and pushed us in the back.

"Sit!" he yelled, then he stormed back around the school building.

"Jackass," I spat toward Bub. Shorty jumped up in my lap and gave his "errf" of agreement.

Bub made a clicking noise with his tongue, "My, my, such language," he said.

Shorty showed Bub his teeth.

Bub drew back against his side of the pickup bed. "Look — a junkyard dog. I'm scared."

Sis climbed into the back of the truck, soda pop in hand, and plopped on the spare tire. She had a keen look of satisfaction on her face.

"Jimmy Jay's little sister told him about the bell, and he told me. I told Dad," she said with a smirk. "He's talking to Mrs. B right now."

"You did what?" Bub said in shock.

My temper was still boiling and I couldn't contain it. I bolted toward Sis, grabbing her long ponytail. In the next instant, Dad appeared and grabbed me by the shoulders. "What in hell's name has gotten into you, Sissy?" he roared as he shook my shoulders. "Well, whatever it is, young lady, I know a cure."

Mama walked up about that time, a look of curiosity on her face. "What's going on?"

Dad didn't answer, and when he stepped into the cab, Mama crawled in on the other side.

Lil Bub ambled up and toppled over the tailgate. He clutched his terrapin and dusty gunnysack in one hand and a giant grasshopper in the other. He held the hopper by the shell of its broad back, and the bug worked its stickery legs and spit tobacco juice trying to escape.

"I'm tard," my little brother said. "Just plumb wore out." Then he let out a loud "wheehh" and made an accidental whistle. His face lit up with a look of surprised delight, and he sat blowing out great puffs, pursing his lips this way and that.

He stopped abruptly, threw back his narrow shoulders, and got a smug look of satisfaction on his face.

"Jimmy told me all about why Shadow and Shorty were stuck together."

All three of us looked directly at our little brother and waited.

"They were sexin," he said with the pleasure of his newly acquired knowledge. "And Shadow's gonna have puppies."

V

Shadow's tummy swelled gradually until her entire appearance changed. Her sly, keen face rounded, and the haunting look in her eyes softened.

The prospect of the coming family filled me with excitement when I thought of them. But for the next several weeks, I didn't have much time to think about anything but work.

Dad didn't switch Bub and me over the bell incident, but before many days passed, I'd have gladly exchanged our punishment for a whipping.

Extra chores didn't describe it. Garden work, weeding the fence rows, scraping and painting gates, and mucking out the barn were just a few of the items on Dad's "list." He had things written on a sheet of tablet paper, nailed to the wall of the shop. When Bub or I would finish one chore and go to the list with a feeling of achievement, Dad would have three new items added.

Every single day, Mama and Dad fought over the punishment. Mama decided after a few days that Dad should let up on us, but my father walked around with a stubborn frown and wouldn't budge.

More and more at night, I'd crawl outside and sleep with my dog on the creek because of my parents' arguing. Each morning when I'd open my eyes to the glory of early summer, smell the sweetness of wild blossoms, and hear the creek, I'd forget the "list" for a few moments.

My mind would linger on my dog, who was always curled next to my neck. I'd think of grand Indian games beneath the trees with Lil Bub, chasing field mice with my dog, and swimming in the pond. I had a particular yearning to get to know Carolyn, who'd moved onto the farm north of us.

After all of those pleasant notions had a chance to get comfortable, I'd sit up and groan with stiffness and reality would return. My fingers had fat water blisters from the hoe, and every muscle tweaked in a different place from my new routines. A cloud settled over my mind when I remembered the endless chores.

More than anything, Dad's list was keeping me from the pressing business of saving money for Mama's car. In spite of everything, Shorty and I had already accumulated a stash. I sold my genuine coonskin cap to a neighbor boy for fifty cents and parted with my best shooting marble for another quarter. I hid the coins in a sock in the bottom of my drawer, and every evening after Sis was asleep and Shorty summoned me outside with his "errf," I'd retrieve the sock and finger the coins in the dark.

Shorty and I would discuss the possibility of making money in new ways. Every time I got quiet, he'd nudge me with enthusiasm and ease my troubled mind.

But every morning when I rolled out of bed and started to work on the list, I felt pressure building. Time was wasting. Summer was going to be half over. Mama and Dad were arguing again, maybe even worse than ever. If I didn't get something to help Mama be happy, she might leave again. Bub's stupid bell idea had cost me.

"Where you goin, Sissy?" Lil Bub asked, running behind me with Shadow at his heels.

"Pick the blackberries."

"Can I come?"

I stopped and checked him over. My brother had been having a lot of sickness, and Mama told him to stay out of the barn and away from the dust. "I reckon you can, but you'll have to stay away from the bushes. They'll be dusty."

"Can Shadow come?" he asked, reaching and scratching behind his dog's ears.

"As long as she stays out of the berry bushes."

Shorty barked his approval. Anywhere Shadow went, he was going to follow.

Halfway to the far pasture, I realized that I'd forgotten to daub myself down with kerosene to discourage the hateful chiggers. I stopped for a moment on the path, decided to forget it, and stomped on.

Three hours later, I walked slowly toward home carrying a full bucket of plump berries. Lil Bub followed while Shorty and Shadow ventured ahead of us for mice.

"Take these up to Mama."

My brother placed a katydid atop the bed of black-berries and took the bucket. "Where you goin now? Ain't we ever gonna play no more?"

"This isn't play. I'm workin on Dad's list." I squinted at him and frowned. He dropped his lower lip and took off toward the house with both dogs following.

My fingers prickled where the berries left tiny stickers. When I dug at the fierce chigger bites, my sun-burned skin tingled with cool pain. I bent my back against the giant scoop shovel and scraped the manure from the barn floor. The fat, green flies stuck to my sweaty arms, and when I slapped them, my arms burned. Mud daubers flashed around my head, and angry swallows darted in and out of the dust-speckled sunlight of the loft.

Later, I stood in the garden looking down an endless row and jerked at pea pods. I straightened, stretched my back, and squinted against the sun. My mood dark-ened when I spotted Bub walking across the barnyard. I knew that he was working hard, too, but he was taking it all so lightly.

My older brother bounced along, slinging his arms, whistling a snappy tune, as happy as if he were headed to the picture show on a Saturday evening.

"Where are you goin?" I barked.

Bub looked at me with amusement, then a look of agony streaked across his face. He fell down in the barn-yard and started crawling toward me, whining with a nasal sob. When he reached me, he grabbed the hem of my ragged shirt and started squalling, "Pleease . . . pleasssee . . . Sissy Boss. Don't hit me! I'm tryin. I just can't get it all done. Pleassee."

"Knock it off," I said, swatting him extra hard. "You aren't funny. This whole mess is your fault." I turned back to my row of peas.

"My, my, what a nasty black mood we're in."

"If you don't get busy and help me, you're gonna cause even more trouble."

"More trouble?"

"Between Mama and Dad. You're gonna make things even worse. All they do now is fight because of us."

Bub looked at me in silence for a long time, and when he spoke, all the fun was out of his voice. "Sissy, don't put things like that in your head. It isn't our fault and we can't make it better or worse. We can't change it."

"Can so."

"Cannot."

"Can so."

"Suit yourself, hardhead," Bub said, walking off. Then he turned.

"Dad said as soon as we finish up what we're doin, we have to start on the peaches."

I stared at Bub's back when he walked away, then returned to my task, roughly pulling the pods, first with one hand and then with the other.

"You don't have to pull them up by the roots," Sis said, coming up from behind, slinging a plastic bucket. I snarled toward her. She had on short, cutoff jeans and sandals, and her slim legs glistened with oil. Her long auburn hair, pinned up in back, was shaded by a wide-brimmed bonnet. She was more serious about a suntan than getting any work done.

"Did Lil Bub go into town with Mama and Dad?" I snapped. "I saw the pickup leave. Are they headed for Ponca to get groceries?" The trip to town once a month for groceries and feed had never appealed to me that much, but that afternoon it irked me that I didn't get a break from work.

"Yes," Sis said, stooping and picking one pod at a time, then brushing the dust from her hands after each effort. "What's with you?"

"You," I blurted. "You and your big mouth, tellin on me and Bub. You and your stupid Miss know-it-all ways."

"My, aren't we testy today," Sis said. At that moment, a car turned in off of the county road. Sis stopped, looked up, and let out a squeal of delight. Jerking her bucket up, she started for the house. "I'm going riding with Francis."

I stared at her in shock. Ever since my sister's friend, Francis, got her driver's license, all Sis talked about was riding to Ponca City.

"What about the peas? Aren't you supposed to help me out with the garden chores?" I felt a hot flush of color rising in my face.

"Poo on the peas. I'm sick and tired of this garden."

"You're gonna cause trouble."

Sis shook her head in disbelief. "Are you still on that mission?" She took a few steps, then turned back. "If you think getting the black-eyed peas picked is going to patch things up between Mama and Dad, you're living in a dream world, little girl."

"Shut up," I said, clamping my hands over my ears.

"Besides that," Sis said, walking back toward me and raising her voice, "I'm only going to be a teenager once." She started off, then turned to make one final point. "You better quit worrying about everyone else and worry about yourself. It's easier and lots more fun."

I swallowed my anger out of necessity. "How much did Francis pay for that car?" I screamed

Sis gave me a puzzled look. "Thousands," she said with a dramatic wave of her hand, then she took off in a skipping jump.

I watched the red convertible disappear down the gravel road. Wiping sweat from my forehead with a dusty hand, I gritted my teeth. Surely Sis was teasing. I thought of the hard-earned $3.85 I had in the sock drawer buried beneath my overalls. The thought of thousands of dollars staggered me with defeat.

"Who needs your help?" I asked out loud, "or Bub's?" I bent back to my work as my dog meandered up. "Shorty, we can save . . . thousands." The word came out with a weak choke and made my mind whirl.

A ripening cornstalk dangled out over the row of peas and tickled my head. I pushed at it once, then twice, but it kept hovering over me. Sun, glare, burn, itch, work, worry, tickle, tickle. I turned savagely and attacked the cornstalk in a rage. I kicked at it with my bare feet, and the stalk swayed and shook, its plump ear of corn bouncing just above my head. I punched at it, but each time it would bounce back, so I'd plunge into it again. In a final, murderous assault, I began to rip the stalk with both hands. The storm of anger didn't pass until the stalk lay flat and the yellow-green ear was stomped into the soft dust.

Shorty, probably feeling like he needed to contribute, walked over, lifted his leg, and sprinkled the defeated stalk.

I stared, dumbfounded. I was even more bewildered when tears squeezed from the corners of my eyes and trickled down my sunburned face. Tears meant defeat. Dad said that tears were a sign of weakness. And Bub said if he could make me or Sis cry, he knew he had us beat. I gritted my teeth, squinted my eyes, and wiped angrily at the dreaded tears. I would never be defeated. Never.

I reached and tried to stand the stalk back up, but it crashed to the ground, broken and lifeless. What could I do to hide it? I tried to pamper it back up, leaning it carefully on its neighbor. Still no good. I knew that Dad would spot the ailing stalk a mile off. The garden was Dad's sacred place. He taught us to respect and cherish the food it gave us. I dropped quickly to my knees and pulled the entire stock up, root and all, and covered the hole. I stepped back to look. If I was real lucky, it might work.

Looking sheepishly toward the barn and praying that Bub wouldn't see me, I carried the cornstalk to the far side of the garden. The summer ground was much too hard to dig. If I tossed the stalk in the creek, the trickle of muddy water wouldn't carry it three feet. Finally, I sprinted the distance to the freshly plowed wheat field. On hands and knees, I dug a deep hole in the soft earth and buried the evidence of my anger.

I was still flushed with guilt when Bub joined me later beneath the peach trees. I reached for the peaches blindly, while my mind kept reeling back to the corn-stalk and why I'd done what I did.

Maybe Sis was actually right. Maybe there really wasn't anything I could do to keep Mama on the farm. The thought burned me with insecurity. My mind leaped to the hideout that Bub had promised to show me. If a divorce did happen, and if the county came to take us away, Shorty and I would need a place to hide.

I'd been mad at Bub ever since the picnic. I hadn't asked him anymore about the hiding place. I climbed into the higher branches of the old tree, sat on a fat limb, and dangled my legs, looking at Bub below.

"They're off to get the groceries, pretty as you ever seen. Off to get the basics— peanut butter, ketchup, and beans."

Bub grinned proudly at his poem. I made it a point not to smile, even though it was funny.

My mind snapped back to the day of the picnic and Bub's words to the teacher — "Sissy did it." In the same instant, I spotted a big rotten peach that was covered with june bugs. There wasn't an inch of that peach I could see — it looked like a living, green ball. The bugs were busy at their task of removing the ripe meat from their treasure.

Bub was just below, balancing himself and his bushel basket on a stepladder, reaching for the peaches on the low limbs. I giggled silently to myself, then inched my way up to the june-bug peach. Ever so slowly, I picked the treasure from the branch, holding it by the fragile stem. Not one of the bugs flew, and I couldn't believe my good luck.

"Wow, look at this beauty. I've never seen a peach so fine," I said.

Bub started looking up, but the sun through the branches caused him to squint and blink his eyes.

"Here, take a look, Bub," I said. "Now get ready — I'll toss it real gentle. Don't miss."

Before Bub had a chance to refuse, I tossed the june-bug peach right into his open hands, and swoosh — those bugs boiled up into Bub's face like angry hornets. Bub squalled and threw the peach high, losing his balance on the ladder. He tumbled to the ground, showered with ladder, basket, peaches, and bugs. Jumping into the air with a howl, he ran backwards, swatting at his ears, stumbling and falling to the ground in a screaming roll. Shorty barked and followed Bub's trail, running around him in wide circles.

I laughed so hard I shook ripe peaches off the tree. I was still hooting and slapping my leg when I saw Bub starting toward me.

"I'm gonna make you eat this peach, Sissy," Bub said. He reached up for me, holding the rotten peach in one hand.

I jumped and took off toward the barn. My breath grabbed in my throat and my heart pounded. I could hear Bub's feet plopping in the dust just behind me. One of his large hands reached out and I went down in a tumble. Bub mashed the rotten peach against my lips. I sat up, spitting and choking with laughter.

"Very funny, Sissy," Bub said. Then a wide grin creased his face. "Actually, it *was* pretty funny," he said. He broke out into a loud, howling roll of laughter. "Pay backs," he said, offering his hand and pulling me to my feet. He gave me a long look of approval. "I guess now it's time for me to keep my end of our bell bargain. If we hurry, maybe we can get to my hideout and return before Mama and Dad get back from town."

Bub took off. I followed, taking two strides for every one of his. He circled around the south end of the farm, crossed the county road, and walked onto the old Osborn place. He started toward the ruins where the house stood, half burned. At the remaining wall, he turned and counted his paces out from the charred building, then fell down on hands and knees and pushed the charcoal dirt with his hands. To my amazement, he soon uncovered a board, then another. He reached and pulled up a splintered door, motioning for me to follow. "Hurry up, before someone comes down the road."

It was a cellar, dark and cool and swept clean as Mama's kitchen. Just as my eyes began to take in the magic, Bub pulled the door shut, drowning us in total darkness. I squeezed my dog tight. Then my brother raked a match across the cement wall and lit two fat candles.

My eyes devoured the scene in front of me through the flickering light. Against one wall was an army cot covered with a red plaid Indian blanket. Next to the bed was a stump table that held a chipped vase of dried red and gold flowers. Reflections bounced off of the wall in the candlelight. Above the bed, two long-bladed, crossed corn knives were hanging. I thought of Robinson Crusoe in the book I'd just read. Rubbing goose bumps from my arms, I took in a ragged breath.

Bub hadn't lied about the place. What a wonderful secret spot for Shorty and me to hide our stash. We could sneak up to the cellar at night and lay our money out and talk about plans to make more. The idea sent my spirits reeling.

"It took a lot of work," my brother said. He pulled open the door of a lopsided wooden cabinet showing off a mixture of canned goods and soda pop. He reached in and pulled out two bottles of red soda pop. Taking his bulky knife from his pocket, he fumbled with its many blades, then popped the lids and handed one to me.

"A person could just live down here, Bub," I said, thinking that it was the perfect place. "How long have you known about it?" I spotted a comic book beside me on the cot. The words glaring at me from the back cover jerked my mind away from the cellar and the conversation. "KIDS, MAKE BIG MONEY."

"I stumbled onto it last summer. It was great fun at first, cleaning it up and bringing my stuff down here. But then the fun kinda went out of it." Bub downed his pop in four continuous swallows, let out a loud belch, and set the empty back on the shelf. "We better get back. If Dad catches us taking a break, we'll probably be slaves for all eternity." I could tell that the idea amused him because a crooked grin sliced across his face.

In the moment after Bub blew out the candle, before he creaked open the cellar door, I hugged my dog tight and told myself, if worse came to worse, we had a place to hide. As long as the cellar remained a secret, we'd never have to leave the farm.

"Bub, can I take this comic book to read, then bring it back?" I had the treasure tucked tightly in my hand.

"Okay."

"Bub?" I asked as we quickly covered the door with the charcoal dirt. "Are you positive no one else knows about this place?"

"Positive. The old Osborn house burned almost five years ago, and this land has never been sold or leased for pasture. Hardly anyone walks by here."

"You won't tell anyone else, will you, Bub?"

"Nope — it's our secret."

"Thanks for showin me. It's perfect," I blurted without thinking.

"Perfect for what?"

For a moment I considered telling Bub about saving up for the car, about my fear of the county and ever having to leave the farm. I quickly dismissed the urge. Bub kept telling me over and over that it wasn't my worry.

"Perfect for what?" Bub repeated.

"Oh, nothing," I said. "Maybe I'll run away some-time."

Bub had been walking in front of me as we talked. He stopped so quick that I bumped into him. He ran his hand through his unruly cotton hair. "I worry about you, Sissy Gal. The ideas you put in that head of yours."

"Don't," I said, feeling a sudden spurt of independence. "I can take care of myself — me, myself, and I."

"You talk about makin trouble," Bub said. "If you ever run away, you better give your soul to God, because your ass will be history if Dad gets hold of it."

I smirked and walked on. The afternoon had rekindled my spirits. I took three running jumps. "Race you to the orchard," I said.

That night, when Shorty scratched below my bedroom window and whined, I looked over to make sure that Sis was in her "sleep lump" with the pillow over her head. Sneaking quietly, I pulled Dad's old railroad lantern from beneath my covers, then crawled out the window and took my dog in my arms.

Near the creek, I sat cross-legged and let Shorty crawl into my lap. "Things are lookin up, buddy. Dad told us this evenin our extra chores are done. We have the rest of the summer to add to our stash." I shook Dad's old lantern until it finally flickered on. I opened the comic book and shined the dim light on the words that I'd read over and over again that afternoon. "KIDS, MAKE BIG MONEY."

Just as I focused my eyes and began to read, Shorty gave me his little "errf" and tugged at my breech leg. "Don't bother me, buddy. We have to read this."

"ERRFF," he repeated, more serious this time. I looked up and could tell by the expression in his eyes that he wanted something. I tried ignoring him one more time by sticking my face back in the comic book.

"ERRFF, ERRFF, ERRFF," he insisted.

"Shhh, you'll wake Dad. Okay, okay, what's wrong? I stood and he bounced away toward the barn. I let the flickering light guide my bare feet down the dusty path. Shorty stopped every few steps, tail wagging, with his eyes focused to make sure that I was still behind him.

He led me to a warm corner on the south side of the barn beneath some straw bales. Before I shined the light, I heard them — tiny voices of new life squeaking against the warmth of their mother's secure bosom.

VI

My heart caught in my throat and pounded as I finally got the puppies in the ray of dim light.

"Oohh," I said, dropping to my knees. "They're beautiful, buddy. Shadow girl, you did good." I counted, touching each one gently as I walked my fingers down the row of squiggly bodies.

"Eight. Eight wonderful puppies, all with shining coats and long legs. Why, they look just like you, girl."

With the words came a tug of disappointment. I'd hoped at least one puppy would be spotted with short, bowed legs like their daddy. "They'll have your heart," I told Shorty, who stood by, his tail in a continual soft wag of pride.

"You have two weeks after they're weaned to give them away," Dad said, standing over the litter as everyone gathered around. He was looking at me when he said it. I wanted to ask what he'd do after that, but I kept shut. The pups would disappear — that was enough incentive for me to get busy.

"Yes, sir," I said, "I'll get started tellin kids about them right away."

"Well, they aren't bowlegged and ugly," Sis said. "They all look just like Shadow."

"They're precious," Lil Bub said, holding a golden-brown pup to his face. "Can't we keep just one?"

But Dad had already turned and left the barn, and I knew that he meant exactly what he said. The fate of the puppies after weaning time would depend completely on me.

That very afternoon, walking the road ditches toward the Nine Mile Corner, I conceived the idea. Those puppies were too good to give away. Everyone at school knew and liked Shorty, and Shadow's reputation for killing snakes had spread throughout Osage County.

"Why, I'll bet those puppies are worth five dollars each." The words burst out of me right in the dusty ditch as I was shoulder deep in Johnson grass. I walked to the side of the gravel road, dropped to my knees, and pulled a sheet of paper and pencil from my overalls pocket. Five times eight — forty dollars! The thought sent my spirits sailing. On the heels of my excitement came the reality that Dad had told me to give them away. Maybe, though, if I was careful, he'd never know the difference.

So I began that day. I walked around to every close neighbor and invited kids to come home with me and see the puppies. It would be much harder for them to resist once they'd held a soft, golden body in their two hands. Then I lied and told each of my potential customers not to mention the five-dollar price tag because I was saving money to surprise my Dad. It amazed me how easy the lie slid out.

The next week, in the midst of my money-making venture, something happened that would turn the rest of the summer into a virtual gold mine.

It was Saturday, and for reasons I didn't understand, Dad decided to take Mama into town alone for the entire day. He allotted all of the Saturday housecleaning chores to Sis and me, then told Bub and Lil Bub to do the yard work.

"Your mother and I are taking a day off. When we return this evening, I want this house shining, supper cooked, and the yard clean as a whistle."

Mama bubbled around the house that morning, dressing in her finest clothes while she gave us instructions on the wash and on frying chicken for supper.

We all waved happily as the two of them, all spit-shined and polished, rattled away in the old pickup truck toward town.

They had barely pulled out of sight when Sis approached me with a strange idea. I looked at her, hesitating.

"Go ahead, choose. I have each room of the house written down. I've made a game of the house chores."

I peeked into the bowl, staring at the slips of paper, then glanced into my sister's green eyes, looking for some dubious motive.

"Come on, let's make it fun. You want to play or not?" she snapped, pushing the bowl under my chin.

The first room I picked was the kitchen. Bad luck. The responsibility of the kitchen held the dreadful job of cleaning the stove, washing and drying all of the dishes, sweeping and mopping the floor, and fixing supper.

I squinted at Sis, wondering how she could possibly cheat. She dipped her hand into the bowl and with too much satisfaction said, "The bedrooms."

Bedrooms were easy. They entailed picking up dirty laundry, dusting, and quickly stripping the sheets.

I peered into the bowl, studying the slips of paper with my eyes. Now I was suspicious of size and shape and wondered why I'd let my sister corner me into her trap. Reaching cautiously in, I grabbed a second slip and tore it open.

"The porch," I squalled, dropping the slip back into the bowl. I glared at Sis. With the porch came the gruesome task of laundry, which included washing, hanging, and ironing. "This isn't fair," I said, knowing that I'd be lucky to finish all of the chores by evening while Sis could breeze through in an hour. "You cheated somehow, didn't you?"

Sis let out a short laugh, and, reaching into the bowl, she took out another slip. "The living room," she sung in a happy song. "Well, we better get started." She shoved the last slip up under my nose. I didn't have to open it. We both knew that it was the dreaded bathroom.

Two hours later, my sister, after floating happily through her chores, drove away with her friend Francis to "drag" Grand, the main street in Ponca City. By six that evening, I was finally putting clean sheets back on the beds and had chicken frying in the kitchen. Every hour that passed that miserable Saturday, I cursed my older sister and swore that I'd find a way to get even with her. First she'd squealed on Bub and me about hiding the bell, causing us weeks of back-breaking chores, and now this.

The very next day, I overheard my sister talking to Bub in the barn.

"Those are the terms — take em or leave em."

"Come on, Sis, give me a break here," Bub said in a pleading voice.

"All of your allowance or I'll tell Dad I caught you smoking." My sister's voice sparked with triumph.

"For how long?" Bub's voice was laced with dread.

"As long as I say."

"You jackass," Bub spit.

"Life's tough," Sis said, her tone sparked with joy.

I sank down behind some bales of hay and let the full impact of my sister's actions soak in.

Late that same night, I lay awake listening to the late summer wind whistle through the trees. Shorty had already scratched beneath my window and whined. I was waiting for my sister to relax so that I could sneak out and go to the cellar to count my money.

Sis, on the opposite side of the bedroom, seemed particularly restless. Finally, she sat up and began slowly rummaging around in the dark. I could see her slipping clothes on and then heard the window by her bed squeak up, inch by inch.

It would take something powerfully important to get her out of bed in the middle of the night. My sister dearly loved her rest. I watched as she opened the window, unlatched the screen, and squeezed out, pulling the window down behind her. Squinting through the darkness, I saw her flick on Dad's lantern and start off toward the creek.

Quickly, I slipped into my overalls and slid out the window, following Sis at a safe distance — down the creek, behind the barn, across the gravel road on the north. The further and faster we went, the more exciting the night adventure became to me. I couldn't imagine what my sister was doing.

Then, in the far distance, I heard the hum of a tractor. Sis stood on her tiptoes and shined the lantern up over her head. The tractor sound grew as it came closer. I ducked behind a tree, not six feet from Sis, and waited.

The new girl, Carolyn, who'd moved on the farm just north of us, had a big brother named Steve. It was his voice that came through the darkness when the tractor pulled to a stop. To my complete surprise, I watched my sister slide easily into Steve's arms, and they kissed.

As soon as the two of them disappeared into the darkness, I skeedaddled toward the cellar. Shorty and I lit one of the fat candles, and I spread the money out on the cot.

"We have nine dollars and fifty cents, Buddy. And I have four puppies promised, so that's twenty. And . . . let me see. Soon our Cloverine Salve should be here." A brief trickle of worry followed the words. I knew that Dad might not approve of me ordering something to sell. But the words from the comic book, "MAKE BIG MONEY," erased the fear. I intended to beat Dad to the mailbox anyway. "Then we have our allowance." The word somehow connected back to Sis and her robbing Bub with her threat.

I stopped what I was doing when a revolutionary thought crashed into my mind. Smothering a giggle, I began to stuff the money back into my sock. Blowing out the candle, I left the cellar, carefully kicking charcoal dirt back over the door. Then I ran home as fast as I could run and returned to my bed.

The next hour, I wiggled and tossed, rehearsing the exact words I would use on my sister. My heart beat with anticipation when I finally heard the gentle squeak of the window sliding upward. I waited until Sis took her clothes off and snuggled warmly into her quilts.

"Wonder what Dad and Steve's parents would say if they knew you and Steve were meeting at night on the creek when he's supposed to be plowing?"

A little gasp escaped Sis and she ripped at the covers, sitting up like she'd been stung by a wasp.

"I want all of your allowance, plus the money you're gettin from Bub. And you can do my share of the house chores for awhile . . . just until I say you can quit."

I genuinely expected Sis to come crashing across the room and land in the middle of me. I said a quick prayer of thanks that Dad had the evening off and was asleep in the next room.

After a few moments of complete silence, Sis said, "Starting when?"

"Tomorrow."

"But that leaves me with nothing. Nothing. No gas money or record money, not even enough to buy a Coke all month in town." The words came out in a whine.

I was grinning from ear to ear in the darkness, a jack-o-lantern of joy, absorbing each second from the nectar of revenge. It took a moment to think of the exact right words to say. "Life's tough," I finally managed, and I even gave the words a bit of my sister's dramatic lift.

There was a squeak and rustle as Sis jumped from her bed and reached for me. She got one hand on my hair.

"Take your hands off of me or I'll scream like a banshee. Then I'll tell Dad everything — your little night meetings with Steve, you bribing Bub out of his allowance, you cheating me into doing all the house-cleaning last Saturday."

Sis let her hand drop and she had such a look of despair on her face, for an instant I almost felt sorry for her.

VII

July came in with blistering days of relentless summer sun. Dad fussed daily about the heat, saying that the fields were scorching. Every evening he studied the sky in hopes of clouds "clabbering up." The arguing between my parents steamed up on those summer nights, sending me and my dog to the far end of the creek and silence.

Sis stayed in a hateful mood, casting devil glances at me anytime I came near. Even Bub became moody and withdrawn, taking a part-time job at the Nine Mile Corner and working in the fields until dark.

A few days before the deadline on the puppies, I became panic-stricken. One by one, I'd succeeded in selling six of Shadow's pups to neighbor kids. Shadow stood by and watched as each child picked a puppy. She would walk up to them and sniff, and then, as if to give her approval, she'd lick her pup one last time and turn back to the others. Shorty would "eerrf eerrf" to the new owner, telling them to take good care of his baby.

Knowing that Dad was in a miserable mood added to the pressure of the two remaining pups.

"Maybe we could hide them somewhere?" Lil Bub offered one afternoon as we discussed our dilemma.

"It would never work. They'd meander back to the house sooner or later to be with Shadow and Shorty. Then Dad would skin us for sure or shoot em."

"Don't you know any other people, Sissy?"

I frowned and thought. I'd walked so far the last four days that my bare feet had blisters between my toes. Most of our neighbors were within ten miles, and after that it became impossible. I'd gone through all of the kids I could think of at school, calling to lure them into a visit.

Then, just as I had worked myself into a state of daily worry, a miracle came my way. One afternoon Dad had several friends that worked with him on the railroad out to test the homebrew from his latest "batch."

After the men had stood out near the shop for several hours sampling the brew, Shadow appeared in the yard with a large snake. She brought the creature toward her two remaining puppies and proceeded to give them "snake-killing lessons." First she'd grab the addled creature by the tail, spin and pop, using her unique method. Then she'd drop the snake, push one of the pups forward with her nose, and continue to urge the puppy until he had a turn at the practice.

The men lined up, leaning on the yard fence and yelling little encouragements to Shadow.

"Hang if that don't beat all," one big man said, drawling out the words, then tipping up his bottle of brew.

"I wouldn't believe it if I hadn't seen it with my own eyes," another slurred.

"That bitch is gifted."

"Only two of those pups left," Dad bragged. "You guys better grab one before you leave today."

And so, I was happy when the two remaining members of Shadow and Shorty's family left to good homes. I had, indeed, lost ten dollars, but it was a small price to pay for knowing that all of the pups were now safe with families of their own. Besides, my savings was growing daily while I enjoyed the leisure of late summer days.

Sometimes when Sis gave me despicable looks, I worried that she'd finally get tired of the blackmail and confess to Dad, but it didn't happen. Not only did she not confess, she continued the night escapades. Each time I'd hear her window squeak open and see the shuffle of clothes in the darkness, I'd smile. It was money in the sock for me.

There was something to be said for having an income with very little effort on my part. It allowed me to bask away in the creek on hot summer afternoons with Shorty and Shadow and Lil Bub. It also allowed a growing friendship to develop between me and the new neighbor girl, Carolyn.

More and more, Shorty and I would traipse up across the field, cross the country road, and visit Carolyn and her dog, Flyboy. I always felt slightly flushed with guilt when Steve spoke to me. I didn't know if Sis had revealed our "arrangement," but I never uttered a word to Carolyn.

That last month of summer, Carolyn and I became best friends. We had wonderful days playing together along the creek, fishing, swimming, and building a hideout beneath the bridge that bordered our two farms. While Carolyn and I played, Shorty and Flyboy searched the weeds for fat mice or chased rabbits across the fields.

As late summer faded, I felt the pressure growing to present Mama with my stash. She and Dad seemed more at odds than they'd ever been. It wasn't just the arguing at night that concerned me. There was a strained silence at every meal, and sometimes Mama would get her faraway look and burst into tears. She needed something to make her happy. And if the money wasn't enough for her to buy a car, at least it was a good start and something that she could look forward to. Every time I thought of the $68.50 in my sock, I beamed with satisfaction.

Only one thing had gone haywire with my money-making scheme, and that was the form I'd filled out and sent in from the comic book. My Cloverine Salve had never come. Every day, I was careful to beat Dad to the mailbox, but as days turned into weeks, finally I gave up and forgot about the Big Money plan.

On a bright afternoon in late August, I went to Bub's cellar to retrieve my money. I'd made some decisions that day. School would soon be starting. Carolyn and I had great plans for turning our bridge into a sacred Indian cave and writing out ceremonies that we could perform. I wouldn't have time to add to my savings during school, and besides, my conscience was pecking at me. It was time to let Sis have her allowance back and Bub have his.

Shorty was with me when I walked into the yard with my bulging sock. I whistled a gay tune, excited to see the look on Mama's face when I dumped the money on the table.

"P Jink, where in the hell have you been?" Dad's voice boomed as the front screen door slammed and he walked toward me across the yard.

I opened my mouth to answer, but he didn't give me a chance.

Dad's face flashed crimson and his eyes narrowed. "I want some answers from you, young lady, and I want them now." He pointed toward the front door. My eyes followed his finger and focused on a huge box setting on the sidewalk.

"That Cloverine Salve came today, addressed to you. What in the world are you doing, sending off for something like that without asking first? And I talked to Katherine Lessert yesterday. She said that Pat and Mike paid five dollars for one of Shadow's pups. Did you sell those pups after I told you to give them away?"

I felt my knees trembling. When the front door slammed again, I saw Mama walking toward us.

"Answer me," Dad squalled, giving my shoulder a shake.

The truth trickled out in little spurts. "I've been workin," I said hoarsely, "picked up pop bottles . . . tryin to make money." I paused and pushed my big toe beneath a peach seed. "I ordered the salve to make Big Money."

"Why?" Dad roared. "Why have you been doing all of this and why lie about it?"

I felt my face flushing. I was cornered. I looked up into Mama's eyes. Shoving my sock out from behind my back, I motioned for my mother to take it. "I did it to help buy Mama a car. I want her to be happy so. . . ."

"So . . ." Dad said, without letting me finish. "SO?" he repeated, looking at Mama. "It's come to this? You want out so damn bad that even the kids are trying to help?"

"I didn't. . . ." Mama tried to explain her innocence.

Dad went into a rage of temper. "Well, fine, wonderful. You can have your way out. We'll get the car. You can have your precious freedom. Come on, we'll do it right now."

When the pickup disappeared in a cloud of red dust, I felt frozen against the ground. I squeezed my bulging sock and felt the slow thumping of my heart beneath my overall strap.

"I heard it all," Bub said, walking up beside me and setting down his bucket of frothy milk.

I stood, paralyzed. Shorty reared up on me and scratched my leg. Nothing but my mind moved. All of my hard work and efforts ripped to threads. Now Dad was so mad and they were fighting and things were worse than ever.

The threat of rain that had earlier rattled and cracked was moving to the south, where it whispered and rumbled with quick flashes of light.

"It isn't your fault, Sissy," Bub said, touching my arm. "I heard it all. It's got nothin to do with you, really."

I couldn't answer. I felt grateful to him for the effort, but Bub's words couldn't calm the storm that raged inside of me. Dreaded tears of defeat began to blur my eyes.

"Of *course* it's her fault," Sis said, walking up to face me and flipping one of my ponytails. "She's been trying to play God all summer, haven't you, little girl?"

"Sis," Bub said, "shut up."

"Make me," Sis said with a smirk. Then she reached for the heavy sock dangling from my hand. "Half of that money is mine. She's been blackmailing me for two months."

Something inside me snapped. I drew back and slammed Sis on the shoulder with the heavy sock, knocking her backward. She came up yanking at my hair and we went to the ground in a heap.

Bub pulled at us until Sis landed a blap across his nose. Then he joined the tirade. Somehow Lil Bub became tangled among our legs, and the churning lump, like a piece of ant-covered candy, shifted across the yard, jerking, swatting, and cursing. Birds flew, bugs ran, and Shorty and Shadow barked in a circle around us until Shadow put Shorty on his back. Our fighting lump worked its way through the back yard and fell in a bruising bump into the stagnant creek.

For a few minutes we all sat, examining our injuries.

Bub spoke first. "So, Sissy, tell me. What have you got on Sis?"

"I caught her sneakin out the window to meet Steve in the fields at night. I got all of her allowance plus what she was gettin from you." I blurted the words out, happy to rub it in.

Sis glared at me, but when she started to move, she gave out a little yelp of pain.

Bub's face slid into his crooked grin, then he began to holler with laughter. He splashed the creek with great slaps, and his booming voice echoed out across the yard. "You deserve that money, Sissy. You keep every cent." Then he got up, still howling, and started toward the barn.

An hour later, I was beneath my willow tree holding Shorty when Dad's pickup rattled down the road followed by an old car. I'd hid my money back in the cellar just to keep Sis from getting it. I had a bad feeling about what Dad intended to do with me when he got home.

Angry voices echoed from the yard into my ears until I put my hands up to block the noise. Then I felt someone standing over me.

"This isn't your fault, Sissy. No matter what happens, you remember that." Bub hesitated. "Mama and Dad want us all at the house."

When Bub and I started in the door, I heard Dad's voice, the anger gone, now choked with emotion. "I lost my temper. Just keep the car, but don't leave today."

"It's too late for that." Mama's words burned into my mind. "Too much has been said. I'm leaving today."

A fear knot seized me by the throat and I stopped on the steps. Bub gave me a little jerk inside, then shoved me toward the kitchen.

Mama looked down at me and wrung her hands. "Sissy Gal, you and Lil Bub can come with me or stay here on the farm with your Daddy."

I couldn't believe her words. The iron clamp of fear tightened. "But Mama, you can't leave the farm again. You promised . . . you . . ."

"Hush, Sissy Gal," Mama snapped.

Bub said, "I'm stayin." Then he disappeared out of the kitchen and I heard the screen door bang.

Sis pushed back the kitchen bench and stood. "I guess I'm staying, too," she said in an aggravated tone. "If you were moving into Ponca, I'd come, but I'm not going off . . . somewhere . . . leave school and my friends." She stopped in the middle of her sentence, let out a little sniff, and ran toward her room.

All eyes turned to me. I couldn't believe what was taking place. In my very worst fears I'd never even considered leaving the farm. I couldn't bear the thought of leaving, yet how could I tell Mama good-bye? I felt like a dusty gunnysack torn between two big dogs.

Lil Bub reached out and clung to my hand with his sticky fingers. "What'er you gonna do, Sissy Gal?"

It was too much. I hit the old screen door running, sprinted out across the yard, and jumped the creek crossing. I ran until my sides throbbed and my breath burned in my aching throat. Then I fell down beneath a thicket of sand plum trees and let the tears flood my face. Shorty joined me, nosing his way up close to my neck. I grabbed him, and the pain in my throat escaped with a sob.

The sky grumbled, rain pelted down in stinging sheets, and lightning streaked, but I didn't move. I wished for a tornado, for blackness, an angry wind to blast down and carry us away.

When I heard Lil Bub's voice calling for me, I stood. My little brother was carrying his baseball bat, dragging it behind him in the mud, leaving a twisted, broken trail. He was taking deep, gasping breaths, and his face stood out pale in the semidarkness of the evening storm.

We started walking in silence back toward home. I wanted to say something, but I didn't know what. I knew that I had to go back with him — get him out of the rain. In that instant, I made my decision. I didn't want to leave the farm. Even the thought tore at my soul. But I just couldn't be separated from my baby brother. I had to do whatever he did.

Shadow came bolting through the storm, and Lil Bub dropped his bat and took her in his arms. He began to hiccup and talk at the same time as the rain let up.

"I . . . love the farm and . . . my Daddy most the best of anything in this world. But I . . . can't let my Mama go drivin . . . off..by her ownself." He grabbed my hand. "W'ater *you* gonna do, Sissy?"

After rubbing my throat three times, I said, "I'm goin with you."

"Good-bye, Shadow Girl," Lil Bub sobbed, wrapping his arms even tighter.

The rain stopped, and in front of us the whole eastern sky colored with a perfect rainbow. I thought of Dorothy in the *Wizard of Oz* — "There's no place like home; there's no place like home."

VIII

Mama stuffed the last of the suitcases next to me in the backseat of the Studebaker as I held my dog tight in my arms.

"I want Shadow, too," Lil Bub said, a pout on his lips.

"Shadow's too big. Besides, she would never be happy in town."

Hearing her name mentioned, Lil Bub's dog appeared and stuck her long nose in the open door, whining at us. Shorty wiggled in my arms. He squeezed out of my grasp and bounced to the ground. Shadow rewarded him with kisses on his nose and chin.

"Let's go," Mama said, climbing behind the wheel and slamming the door.

"Come on, buddy." I slapped my leg.

Shorty looked at me, his soulful eyes liquid with regret. My heart stopped. "No, you can't stay," I said in a hoarse whisper. "Come on, buddy, we have to go."

Shadow whined at him and gave him more kisses, as if to remind him that she was the true love of his life. Jealousy sliced through me, and for an instant I hated Lil Bub's dog.

Shadow bounded away, toward the creek, then stopped and gave a barely audible whine. With one last look of remorse, my dog turned and started after his friend.

"Shut the door, Sissy. He wants to stay with Shadow, so that's that."

"But — I . . ." My mind whirled with the reality of Shorty's decision. I wanted to run after him — to hold him tight and make him go with me. He'd be sorry later on that he stayed.

Mama gave out a long sigh of exhaustion, opened her door, slammed the back door, got in, and put the car in reverse.

My emotions scattered like dandelion seeds in a March wind as Mama pulled the Studebaker down the gravel road toward the highway. My dog had a mind of his own. It wouldn't have been right for me to force him to go. I understood that he'd worry about Shadow. But how could he say good-bye to me?

That night, lying in the backseat among the boxes, staring up at the yellow August moon, I hated everyone. I hated Mama for breaking her promise about leaving the farm. I hated Dad for not trying harder to stop her, Sis for her big mouth, and Bub for disappearing and not saying good-bye. When I tried to hate my dog, the tears started.

The tears came in a great torrent, and I couldn't control them. I cried quietly, letting the gush drench my cheeks, then roll down my neck and onto the seat. When the pain became too much, I put myself in another place and another time.

That week, I'd read a story about the Cherokee Indians and the terrible journey that they made from their homeland in North Carolina to Indian territory. The Trail of Tears it was called. I put myself in the moccasins of a Cherokee girl, walking on the long journey. The white soldiers were around us, forcing us onward. My father had been killed when he tried to resist the journey. My mother was grieving and my baby brother ill. Every step I walked away from my homeland, my heart grew heavier.

The tears finally stopped, and in their place was a quiet resolve. No matter how far Mama drove away from the farm, my homeland, I would return. I would soon be back to the creek and the trees and the animals with my dog snuggled against my neck. That thought gave me a quiet strength to survive.

Soft sounds came from the front seat, and I sat up in the darkness. The moonlight sifted in through the windows, and I saw Lil Bub sleeping in a tight knot, his head in Mama's lap. I watched for a moment in the darkness as Mama dabbed her eyes with a Kleenex. I didn't understand my mother. She wanted to leave, but now she was unhappy.

"Mama, where are we goin?" I snapped.

She jumped and the car swerved. "Sissy, you frightened me. I thought you were asleep."

"Are we leavin the homeland forever?" I wanted answers — some assurance that this trip wasn't one way.

After a long silence Mama said, "We're going to Arizona to visit my brother, your uncle."

"When are we comin back?"

"We're just . . . going on a little vacation, that's all."

I flopped back into the seat and tried to fix the U.S. map in my mind. I wished that geography had been one of my better subjects. How many states were between Oklahoma and Arizona?

Thinking of school brought a spurt of hope. It was late August. School would start in just two weeks. I'd have to be back for school. But sometimes when Mama left, she'd been gone for months. The thought made my stomach gurgle.

My fingers were exploring the underneath side of the seat as I thought. I found a loose thread in the upholstery and began to pull. Soon a small hole emerged beneath my fingers and I yanked. I took my fingers and wallowed them around, making the hole bigger. I hated the car. It was the reason why we were leaving. Then I hated myself. How stupid I had been — thinking that I could stop Mama from leaving by getting a car.

I took my feet and pushed against the boxes until things squeaked and groaned.

"What are you doing back there?" Mama finally said.

I awoke the next morning to the sound of Lil Bub's sneezing. The sun was scorching through the side window and I was thirsty. The car smelled stuffy, and the air was hot and stale. I wished for the back of the pickup with the wind in my face.

When I sat up, the scenery shocked me. There wasn't anything in sight but the winding blacktop ahead of us — nothing but miles of empty sand. I instantly missed the shade of the giant cottonwoods and the sweet tickle of my willow tree above soft grass.

My tummy rumbled and a dead taste began to boil in my throat. Sweat popped out on my forehead and my belly rolled. I jerked both hands over my mouth and groaned.

Mama pulled to the side of the road, and I ripped the car door open just in time. I stumbled out, fell down on my knees, and puked in the road ditch. The vomit stuck to the ends of some weeds and strung out in the dusty wind.

When Mama helped me back to the seat, everything was spinning. I felt like I'd been riding upside down on the merry-go-round. I clamped my eyes shut, but the horrid dizziness continued.

By that evening, I wanted to die. The car sickness wouldn't let up. I finally managed two sips from a soda pop only to lose the liquid less than ten minutes later in the paper sack between my knees. I tried putting myself back in the Indian girl's moccasins — tried walking again on the Trail of Tears — but it was no use. I just wanted out of the car. I ached to be outside in the open air near the creek, walking with my dog.

We drove on and on. When the last of the evening light faded pink behind the hills, I lay, cursing beneath my breath.

Lil Bub started his prayers from the front seat.

"Now I lay me down to sleep . . . and God bless Mama and Dad and Bub and Sis and Sissy Gal and Shadow and Shorty."

"He's not listenin," I said.

"Sissy Gal," Mama scolded.

I stuck my tongue out in the darkness with a quick thrust. Then I did it again and again, like a snake cornered in a bucket. I continued the hateful gesture until my tongue gave out and my jaws began to ache.

The next morning I awoke to the sound of my brother's shrill voice.

"Look, Sissy, look at them hills. I ain't never seen nothin like em before. And them giant cedars."

Mama gave out a chuckle. "Those aren't hills, Lil Bub. They're called mountains. The trees are Ponderosa pines."

I looked out the window and rubbed my eyes in disbelief. It was like God had picked us up out of the endless sand and dropped us into paradise. I cracked a window and sucked in the freshness of the crisp, cool air. It was filled with a brisk dryness new to my senses. I tilted my head, trying to see the tops of the towering trees. Looking down, I could see a car winding below as small as a piss ant. The altitude made my head begin to spin.

"Are we close to Uncle's house?" Lil Bub asked, bubbly with excitement.

I waited to hear the answer, aching to be out of the car.

"We're here," Mama sung out. "Happy Jack Lumber Camp."

A cozy town appeared in the distance. Log houses were scrunched close together back against the mountainside. Smoke twisted up from every chimney, and the giant stack from a lumber mill bellowed. The sound of a cutting blade zipped against logs in the quiet morning, and the smell of wood smoke drifted into my nose.

"I just want to explore. I won't get lost. Please?"

"Sissy Gal, you've already been told a dozen times, you can't go outside the yard," Mama said. "Now go watch tv with your brother."

I dragged myself back to the spot in front of the television set and dropped to the floor with a thud. I didn't look at the tv though. Instead, with a darting glance, I looked around me in the small house. Things were pushed and shoved into every corner until the house sat like a fat hog in a crate. The feeling of being squashed in the small house, trapped inside the tall board fence, created a growing restlessness in me.

I missed the open, airy rooms of home. The hardwood floor streaked with morning sunlight, squeaking with emptiness when I tiptoed across. The windows open wide and the soft curtains blowing in the wind drifted through my mind.

"Lil Bub, let's go do somethan in the yard," I insisted, pulling on his sleeve.

"Leave me alone, Sissy," he said, swatting at me.

I sighed and started for the door. My brother seemed hypnotized by the black-and-white screen. I had to admit, the tv. held a certain magic the first few days of the visit. But after a week, I could barely sit in front of it without squirming. My mind would no longer focus on the moving pictures or sound coming from the strange box. Instead, my thoughts pulled me back to the homeland and the many miles that separated us.

Outside, I walked the backyard in pacing strides. The fence that Uncle had around his yard was like a fort. I couldn't peek through it or over it. There wasn't one private corner where I could do my Indian ceremonies — no feathers and no pokeberry juice for paint.

I would sit for hours cross-legged and think of the Cherokees and how misplaced they must have felt in Oklahoma. How they must have yearned for their North Carolina homeland. I thought of their brave attempts to outrun the white soldiers and how some of them fought and died trying to return home. I wanted to die and come alive in a different time so that I, too, could fight.

"Sissy," Uncle said, walking out into the yard, "don't miss the ice-cream man today. It's Friday." He handed me a nickel.

I thought of the musical truck singing down the mountain and kids boiling out into the street. What fun it had been the week before. I forced a half smile. Taking the nickel, I stuck it into my overalls pocket.

"Thanks."

"Tell me about your farm," Uncle said, brushing pine needles from the ground and sitting next to me. "What's it like this time of year, in autumn?"

The question warmed me with a flood of memories. "Well, it's harvest time. We dig potatoes and pull and hang the onions. The leaves on my willow tree turn to soft gold, and the maples go silver. All of my animals begin to put on their fluffy coats. It's me and Shorty's best time on the creek at night."

"You miss your dog and the farm, don't you?"

The question brought such a flood of homesickness that I felt my insides inflate like a balloon until I ached from head to toe. Tears boiled up in my eyes, but I blinked them back and allowed them to fall inside, in my soul.

The terrible yearning to return home grew with every passing day. I would sit behind the tv in the cramped house until I had to bolt out into the yard and run around and around the fort fence.

Brutal returned to my dreams, chasing me until my legs ached. But I refused to go to Mama for help. Instead, I'd go alone into the small bathroom and sit quietly in the tub with a quiet trickle of warm water. Then I could close my eyes and carry myself across the miles, to the creek, with Shorty cuddled against my neck.

The second week of September, I sat in the tiny bathroom, my face buried in a book of Indian history. Reading became my salvation and the bathroom my retreat. With the door locked, I'd sit beneath the sink with the water trickling. Lost in the grip of the Battle of the Little Bighorn, Shorty would be beside me, near the creek, living the drama one word at a time.

Every day Lil Bub began to say, "We'll probably be goin home in the mornin." I would rub his back and mess his orange knots, because I had a nagging fear about the prediction. I wasn't sure why the gloom first settled on me, but when it happened, my desire to leave Arizona turned into a jagged knife of pain.

I began to think about running away. I thought of darting off into the thick forest with my bundle of food tucked under my arm. I'd get help from the nearby Navajo Indians — maybe live with them awhile in their tiny villages and learn their ways. They'd send me toward home with great ceremony, riding a fine spotted pony.

One afternoon as I left the bathroom and was headed out to check on my little brother, I stopped abruptly in the hallway when I heard my aunt's voice.

"We can enroll Sissy Gal in Flagstaff. She should be in school."

"Well, then," Mama said, "we'll get that done tomorrow."

The terrifying truth sifted over me. I slammed my hands over my ears, refusing to believe what I'd just heard. We weren't going home. We were staying. We were going to live in the stuffed house with the pine-needle yard. I bolted out into the light of the kitchen.

"You're a liar," I said, choking the words out of my throat. "You said we were on a vacation. I'm not stayin here. I want to go home. Shorty and I have to go to school at Braden."

Mama hung her head, then looked up into my angry eyes. "Sissy Gal, I've changed my mind. I'm sorry. I've decided that you should go to school here . . . just for a little while."

I gave my mother a squinted stare. Even though I'd secretly feared the truth, I wouldn't accept it. Shorty would be lost when I didn't come home for school. He wouldn't know what to do. If he followed Bub and Sis, they'd be catching the high-school bus. I pictured my little dog standing in the field, howling out his confusion and sorrow.

My anger surged when I felt tears threatening. I walked slowly through the house and into the yard, opened the forbidden gate, and started to run.

I dashed down the side of the giant mountain, through the pines. Birds darted, squirrels chattered, pine needles flew. I ran until my throat ached and my heart throbbed painfully. Then I slumped beside a fallen tree and shivered in the coldness.

Running away was a fantasy. I knew it, staring up at the snow-covered peaks. I could tell already that winter in the mountains was much different than winter at home. I couldn't leave my little brother, and he couldn't take the cold that sifted in every evening with the setting sun.

I heard footsteps crunching.

"Mama told me," Lil Bub sobbed, mopping his face with the back of his sleeve. "Oh, Sissy, I wanta go home. What will become of Shadow? She's gonna forget me."

I felt the iron grip of pain clamp my throat as I took my brother's hand. "No, she won't. Dogs are like elephants — they never forget."

"How da ya know?" he asked, lifting his wet face. "Did Bub tell ya?"

"Yes," I lied, "Bub told me." I knew that the words would bring him some relief, because Lil Bub considered our older brother an expert on everything.

A thousand fears swarmed through my mind like hornets. How long would Mama keep us in Arizona? What would the strange school be like? Would Shorty and Shadow be okay on the farm, or would Dad take a notion to haul them off, or . . .?

My uncle was lifting Lil Bub up and reaching to take my hand. "Let's get back to the house and have some nice soup. It's getting cold out."

I refused to move. "We're not stayin," I said. "I don't know what I'm gonna do, but we're not stayin."

Uncle let out a long sigh. "I know that this is difficult, Sissy, but it will all turn out for the best. God loves you."

I glared at him. Jerking away from his grasp, I stomped toward the house, pulling my little brother along.

"God doesn't even know where I'm at," I said, and when the words gave me a spurt of relief, I screamed them. "God doesn't even know where I'm at!" My shrill voice echoed up through the trees and above the distant sound of the lumber mill.

IX

After two weeks, I still stumbled around the large school building, frightened and confused. When the bell rang, I always had a moment of fear. Could I get to my locker, remember the combination, and find the next classroom in time? Would I walk in after the tardy bell again? See the disapproving look of the teacher and the haunting black eyes of the mostly Indian students?

Everything about the school was a nightmare. Ninety percent of the students were Navajo Indians, nearly black with piercing ebony eyes. When I tried talking to them, they did nothing but stare. After many futile attempts at friendship, I gave up, not blaming them. I had too much empathy for the Indians. I didn't blame them for hating white people.

"Hey, Okie," a voice cut sharp across the hall. "You lost again?" I ducked quickly into the girl's bathroom — my one retreat. It was a mistake. Four large Indian girls were leaning lazily against the wall, smoking. The smoke filled the room with choking irritation, and when I put my books on the sink, I made the mistake of coughing.

"Oh," one of the girls said, "farmer girl not like smoke." A muffled chorus of snickers echoed from mirror to sink to wall."

"I do, too. Back home in Oklahoma I build fires and do Indian rituals with smoke." I said the words proudly.

None of them laughed, but amusement danced in their black eyes. "White girl wants to have dark skin," one of them chided.

I marched quickly toward the bathroom stalls and shut the door. I could hear their whispers and saw moccasined feet. When I finished and tried to pull the door open, I knew what they were doing.

The tardy bell rang. I jerked on the door with all my might, but it wouldn't budge. When the last bell rang, the moccasins disappeared silently. I finally got the door open, grabbed my books, and ran out into the empty hall. Which room was I supposed to be in? Music! I tore down the hall in a noisy clatter toward the music room.

The room was empty. A panic seized me. What day was it? Oh god — Friday. It was dance day. I'd been told to wear a dress and soft-soled shoes. I looked down at my faded overalls and boots. I couldn't wear boots on the gym floor. What kind of socks did I have on? Any holes?

I dropped my books in the empty classroom and dashed toward the gym. Pulling open the heavy dual door, I quickly jerked off my boots and ran for the circle of kids, my face burning.

I was thankful for the loud music that had already begun and that the teacher didn't scold about my overalls and stocking feet.

"Okay, boys in one line over here," teacher chirped. "Girls over here. For the first dance, boys pick a partner."

I felt an immediate relief. No one would pick me. For all of the sporting events I longed to be a part of, no one ever picked me. I always ended up alone on the bench. Although it was usually embarrassing, this time it would be a relief. It was better than getting out in the middle of the huge floor dressed different than every other girl. Besides, I knew nothing about formal dancing and had no desire to learn. The only dances that I yearned for were Indian dances where I could strip down to my bare skin and call out words from the deepest part of my ownself.

As the line dwindled, I grew impatient. I wished that they would hurry so I could slide off in the corner, unnoticed.

When I saw the giant feet in front of me, I let my eyes travel slowly upward. The biggest Indian boy in the entire school was in front of me, hand extended. I swallowed. How could I refuse? My white hand disappeared into the darkness. All eyes were on me, and I heard a muffle of snickers as I walked with my partner toward the dancing circle.

The music began. The giant took a slow, deliberate step with a thud that seemed to shake the walls of the gym. I chanced one quick look up the brown mountain to the dark face. I stumbled, and the giant's foot came down with a slam. He caught the tip end of my worn sock beneath his toe. I jerked my foot, and when I did, the sock slid off and lay, gray and limp, on the hardwood floor. Someone yelled. Another pointed. The laughter began. It came slowly, like distant thunder moving shyly over the hills. Then it thundered, filling the gym, echoing off of the walls.

The teacher tried once, twice, to swallow her laughter, then exploded into a hooting guffaw. The giant, just as the fun started to die, bent and picked up the anklet, holding it in the air like a dead mouse. The very rafters of the room rang with hysterical howls.

I stood, head down. I tried with every fiber of my being to muster some spark of fight, but anger toward the Indians was something that I could not achieve. I blinked back tears and swallowed with a dry gulp. My mind went to Cootie, shivering beneath the steps of Braden School.

I closed my eyes and prayed to be dead. It was a sad thing to lose spirit. I turned quietly and left the gym floor amidst the chaos of laughter. I was no longer Sissy Gal, running free in my homeland. I was Okie — lost and afraid.

That evening at supper, I couldn't choke down one bite of food. My aunt grabbed me up and squeezed me into warm arms, trying to lift my spirits with her laughter. I sat like a statue and glared at my mother. If I was going to be miserable, I decided that at least she would know about it.

More and more, I became lost in my Indian rituals and fantasies. It was a way for me to remove myself from the pain and return to the homeland in my mind. I had two treasured chicken feathers that Lil Bub had confiscated for me while playing with a friend down the road. They were with me always.

In the backyard, I would place the feathers in my hair, sit cross-legged, and close my eyes. With practice and concentration, I could actually return to the creek and be beneath my willow tree. Shorty would be warm against my neck, and I could hear his breath and smell the crisp autumn fields and hear the creek trickling.

At school, the minute I stepped into the building, I'd head for the bathroom. Taking the feathers from their secret place in my English book, I'd fasten them securely in my braids. At first, some of the big girls pointed and chuckled behind their hands.

"I understand your hatred of me," I would say in a toneless manner. "I accept it completely." That usually brought a few raised eyebrows but no comment. Perhaps I amused them or else they thought me completely loco. Either way, I began to blend into the bigger scheme of things.

Crisp days of autumn turned quickly into winter. Snow began to fall. It drifted down day after day in soft flakes as big as quarters. I felt like I was being spun inside a white cocoon. I wanted the whiteness to smother me and kill the aching homesickness. The pain was no longer inside. It spread all the way outside of my heart onto my skin and hurt me anytime I moved or thought or breathed.

On Thanksgiving, a letter arrived from home, and Lil Bub and I read every word over and over. Bub wrote about his new FFA jacket and told Lil Bub that Shadow was fine. Sis wrote about a new boyfriend from Fairfax, and Dad put a few lines at the bottom about missing us and wanting us all to come home.

Bub scratched a P.S. at the bottom.

SHORTY IS LOST WITHOUT YOU. HE WALKS WITH SIS AND ME EVERY DAY TO THE END OF THE FIELD. WHEN WE CATCH THE HIGH-SCHOOL BUS, HE LOOKS LOST. HE'S ALWAYS THERE IN THE AFTERNOONS WAITING, LIKE HE THINKS MAYBE YOU WILL STEP OFF THE OLD BUS.

His words caused a barb in my throat that hung like a burr to a pant leg. And for days, the sticker pricked my heart each time my mind traveled home to Shorty. It was exactly as I had imagined. My dog didn't understand, and he was sick inside the same as me.

For a week, I wrote a long letter every day to Shorty. I addressed the five-page volumes to my brother, asking him to read them out loud to my dog. I assured Shorty that I'd return soon and told him not to worry. I even shared stories of the Indian battles I'd been reading about. Finally Mama refused to mail the fat envelopes, saying that she wasn't working yet and had no money for stamps.

Christmas turned to January, and February roared into March with frigid winds and subzero temperatures. A strain of bad flu hit the small mountain community, and I came down with it.

My days turned into a confusion of feverish dreams and heat-flashed chills, doses of coal oil and sugar. I lay on the bottom bunk beneath my brother and shivered with rattling teeth at the sound of the icy wind against the windows.

Each time I opened my eyes, it was dark. When I closed my eyes, I was haunted by Brutal. I had a nightmare of being Cootie Brown, shivering beneath the steps of Braden School. Shorty would be wandering around the school grounds, whining and crying. I would call to him and he'd come look under the porch, but he wouldn't know me. On the outside I looked like Cootie Brown, but on the inside I knew that I was Sissy Gal. Yet my own dog didn't recognize me.

Many times the cornstalk from the garden would be part of my dreams. I'd be swatting and slamming it until it wilted to the ground, then I'd be running and running with Brutal on my heels. I'd wake up mumbling, "There's no place like the homeland — no place like the homeland."

When the fever finally broke, I sat up in bed and pulled the blinds back with trembling fingers. I was weak and dizzy and had a terrible, dead taste in my mouth.

"She's up," I heard Lil Bub's shrill cry. Then he was bouncing on the edge of the bed, reaching for my hand. "Get all better, Sissy Gal."

My aunt brought me a steaming bowl of chicken broth with salty crackers. I took one nibble of cracker and two sips of soup and felt full. "Bless your heart — you've had a tough time of it," she said, patting my hand.

When Mama sat on the bed, I turned my face toward the window and lifted the blind. "The homeland," I said. "The creek is icy now and the pond frozen."

"Honey, you have to quit all this . . . imagining stuff."

"Want homeland," I said.

Later that evening, I got up to go to the bathroom and heard Mama's voice from the living room in the semidarkness. "I'm real worried about her," my mother said with a sniff. "She lives more and more in this imaginary Indian world of hers. I don't think she's going to adjust."

I snuggled back into the bed, and Mama's words circled in my mind. I drifted off into a peaceful sleep. I dreamed I was sitting in the pine-needle yard with my feathers when, in the far distance, I heard something in the sky. It was just a speck, and at first I thought it was a wild goose, lost from its flock. With heart pounding, I jumped up and screamed in joy. It was Fob. He landed gently on the tall fence and beckoned for me to join him.

With a feeling of complete ecstasy, I slid easily onto the soft bird back and tangled my hands in his fox fur.

Almost instantly we were back in Oklahoma, approaching the farm. I could see the old schoolhouse and the farm below with the creek snaking around behind our house. I searched desperately for a small brown-and-white speck. "Shorty!" I began to call.

"Shorty!" Fob joined me, his voice singing the word happily. "Shorrtttyyy."

I awoke with a jump, my heart flopping wildly inside of my chest. It was the first time that Fob had visited my dreams for a long time. He had come to me for a reason.

The homeland by spring. Soft green of new grass, romping with Shorty in the cool creek, playing in the alfalfa with the butterflies. I'd run free, as far as my feet would carry me, my face to the wind, and at night, I'd cuddle my dog beneath the willow tree. Fob had whispered the secret into my soul.

Desire rattled through me like a tornado wind against a cellar door. Mama's words came crashing back into my mind. "I don't think she's going to adjust."

"Thank you, Fob," I said out loud in the darkness.

Hope raged inside my mind, causing my breath to come in quick, short gasps. I was going home. Home to the booming thunderstorms, the warm wind, and the trickling creek. Home to the night games on the water in the moonlight holding my dog. HOME.

X

Mama announced her new part-time job at the country store nearby, but it didn't discourage me. I had a quiet peace inside the deepest part of me. I would be home by spring. My mind, however, raced toward possible ways to get the plan into action.

My first day back to school, I sat on the steps and looked out over the snow-packed playground. The Navajos were practicing for their spring baseball season. "Baseball and the number-one team," that's all I'd heard for weeks. But anytime I tried to play, the kids ignored my efforts and left me sitting on the bench, as if I were invisible.

"What would Bub do?" I wondered, thinking of his bell scheme and all of the aftershocks. A smile flickered across my lips, and I stood and edged my way toward the ball field. A few dark eyes followed me. If I could make them mad enough to fight — if we got into a real knockdown drag-out — maybe Mama would be afraid to send me back. By and by, she'd worry about me not going to school. Then she'd have to let me go home.

When I saw the pitcher release the ball, I could see that it was going to fall short. I darted in front of home plate, swooped down, and caught the ball on the run. I turned, stuck out my tongue to the bewildered pitcher, and took off around the school building.

Although the Indian students had never actually threatened to hit me, I knew from their eyes that my only salvation had been the straight-lipped principal and my decision to remain close to the building during recess. I was giving them an opportunity they'd waited for. I heard the footsteps of some of the bigger boys directly behind me as I ran. When someone jerked my pigtail, I turned around, clinging to the baseball.

The muscular boy held out his dark hand for the ball. I dug back into Bub's vocabulary and a nugget flashed into my head. If I could only make them fighting mad.

"Blanket ass," I snarled as he tried to pry the ball away. Then I wallowed my tongue, spit with all my might, and was immediately satisfied when the wad hit the boy just above the eye.

A hard blap crashed across my nose. I heard a chaos of grunts and started swinging my fists. Someone caught me with a hook that knocked me to the ground. I began to wail at the top of my lungs and was relieved when I spotted the principal walking fast toward the circle of dark faces that towered over me.

After a short while in the principal's office, Mama showed up. Her face went aghast at the sight of me. I opened my good eye slightly, then began to moan. The wet cloth against my bloody nose oozed, and I dropped it with a splat at Mama's feet.

"My god, what is the meaning of this? Isn't there any supervision up here? I can't . . ."

"Ma'am, I assure you, it won't happen again. I can't imagine what took place, but I can assure you . . ."

"Ooohhhh." I put my head in my hands. "Want homeland."

The next morning when the bus pulled up and honked, I didn't stir from the kitchen table.

"Run on now. It'll be okay," Mama said. "The principal promised me."

"Want homeland," I grunted, shaking my head. They were the only two words that I'd uttered for weeks.

"You jump and run — the bus is waiting."

I didn't budge.

Mama stood up and jerked off her soft house slipper. Lifting me out of the chair by the arm, she swatted me twice on the bottom.

The surprise display of anger startled me at first and confused me enough that I started for the door. But when I saw the yellow bus squeaking to a stop, I knew that I couldn't get on. Not only would it ruin the first part of my plan to return home, but the Indians had been grounded from baseball because of the fight. If I stepped on that bus, I could kiss the world good-bye. The reality of the situation hit me. I reached for the doorknob and took a death grip with both hands.

Mama swatted my hands with the slipper and tried to pull me loose, but I clung like a turtle to a tadpole. She finally dropped the slipper and began to jerk on me. As fast as she'd pull one hand free, I would grab back with the other. Finally she stomped back toward the kitchen, mumbling a colorful string of swear words.

An hour later, Mama came to me in the bathroom. I sat cross-legged, my two feathers dangling from my hair and my face streaked with some of Lil Bub's finger paint.

"Sissy, you have to stop this," Mama started in a patient tone. "I know you aren't that happy, but you must try. All this . . . Indian stuff. And fighting at school. I don't know what to say to you anymore."

"Want homeland," I grunted.

"Well, we aren't going back to Oklahoma, so you might as well adjust." She stood, wringing her hands, and walked out the door.

Her words didn't deter me. My spirit had returned and nothing Mama could say would daunt my efforts to go home. I refused to even think of her words. Instead I closed my eyes, turned the water on in the sink, and took myself back to the Trail of Tears. I became an angry young brave. I had convinced my fellow Cherokees to rebel against the white soldiers. One by one we annihilated the enemy, gathered our things, and returned to the homeland. In a glorious ceremony I was honored by the chief.

"Sissy, what are we gonna do? I wanta go home."

When I heard my little brother's voice, I raised my head and opened my eyes.

"We are."

His eyes sparkled with excitement. "Really, Sissy, how do you know?"

"The spirits have brought me the message in a vision."

"Can I do anythang to halp?"

His words opened up a new realm of possibility, adding to my solid determination. "Maybe. But it would have to be our secret. You couldn't tell Mama."

"Cross my heart and hope to die," Lil Bub said, quickly marking his chest with his index finger. "Tell me what to do."

"Later," I said. "After the spirits have spoken to me in my dreams."

That night at supper, when Lil Bub pushed his food around on his plate, Mama got a worried look on her face.

"I hope that you aren't coming down with Sissy's flu. What's happened to your appetite?"

Her words were like a flash in the darkness. My mind whirled with new possibilities. The minute supper was over, I drew my brother into the bathroom.

"You have to get sick," I told Lil Bub.

"What?"

"If you want to help me with your plan, you have to act sick. Don't eat much. Whine, cough, and sneeze. You know — be sick."

My little brother wrinkled his nose in disbelief. "You sure this is gonna work?"

"The spirits have spoken," I grunted. "We must answer."

That same evening, at bedtime, Mama brought a stack of books in and plopped them on the foot of the bunk bed. "I got your lessons today from school. We'll try this for awhile and see if it works out. Your teachers have the assignments marked."

When she paused to hear my prayers, I let out a string of Indian sounds and motioned in midair with my hands.

Mama stared at me, dumbfounded.

From the top bunk, Lil Bub went into a hysterical fit of coughing that ended in a sneeze and a hiccup.

"I better get you some medicine," Mama said after putting her hand to my brother's forehead.

"If I have to eat coal oil and sugar, your 'spirits' better know what they're talkin about," Lil Bub whispered to me.

"Trust me," I said.

The next evening at supper, Lil Bub was sitting over his plate, looking at the food in disgust. I'd been sneaking food from the kitchen for him to eat before supper so that we could con Mama into thinking he was very sick.

"I wanta go home," Lil Bub said, looking first at Mama, then casting a quick glance at me.

I felt a streak of fear slide through me. If he spilled the beans, I'd get the worst spanking of my life and probably would have to live in Arizona forever. I jumped up and grabbed the thick Bible from its place on the floor near Aunt's chair.

"God loves us and wants us to be happy," I started in an inspired tone. I hugged the book to me just like I'd seen Grandma Carrie do.

"Just pray with me, Lil Bub. If it's God's will, He will take us home."

My mother stopped her fork in midbite and looked at me with a paralyzed stare. It was more words than I'd spoken in her presence for three months.

A week later, my little brother and I were still conspiring.

"My allergies," Lil Bub said, his eyes lighting up.

"But you haven't had much problem with them since we got here," I said. "What are some of the things that stir them up?"

"Dust and chocolate."

The idea definitely had merit. I glanced out the window. The snow had finally quit falling, but the ground was still covered. Winter in the mountains lasted forever. "We don't have any chocolate, and there sure isn't any dust."

The next morning, we watched as Mama walked out of the yard toward her job at the store and Uncle took his wife to town. As soon as the cars disappeared down the winding road, I ran through the house jerking up throw rugs.

I squeezed past my brother with a bundle of dirty rugs and slammed the bathroom door. We both began to shake, and a fog of choking dust filled the air. I coughed and shook harder, closing my eyes against the rising cloud.

"Hey, yaw, hey yaw," I chanted, dancing in a circle.

Lil Bub opened his mouth wide and breathed deeply. "Shadow girl," he choked, "I'm comin home."

"He's been doing so good," Mama said that night at the supper table. "I just don't understand it."

I cast a guilty glance at Lil Bub, who sat rigid at the table, congested, his eyes red and swollen. I felt a moment of grief for his suffering, but like me, he was willing to do anything to return home.

The first day of March, I walked into the little country store nonchalantly. Lil Bub and I decided that chocolate bars would work better than dust, and at least he'd have the pleasure of eating them. I strolled casually into the store that afternoon, scared almost to death.

"Your mother's already gone," the owner said, leaning over the mahogany counter.

"Oh," I said, acting surprised. "Well, I'll just warm up a bit, then walk back." I ambled down the aisle, taking note of the contents of the crowded, dusty shelves. When my eyes located the chocolate bars, I turned a quick, guilty glance backward.

Stealing was a new concept for me. A shudder of memory traveled through my mind. Dad caught Bub and his friend Larry Gene stealing watermelons from a neighbor once. He strapped poor Bub until he peeled hide, then gave him double chores for three months.

This was different. It was stealing for a good reason. I reached out and snatched two thick bars of chocolate and stuffed them into my coat pocket. I felt my face redden as I turned to dart out the door. The storekeeper's polished shoes gleamed in front of me. My eyes traveled upward. Fear shot through me and I started to dart out the door, but a bony hand came down and grabbed the collar of my coat.

"You young rascal. What do you think you're doing?" The man didn't wait for an explanation, but instead towed me outside and down the block toward Uncle's house. The old man hammered loudly on the door with his closed fist.

My mind was spinning with thoughts, but I couldn't come up with an excuse that sounded reasonable.

"I caught this brat stealing from me," the storekeeper squalled when Mama came to the door.

"Let go of her," Mama said, snatching me away from the accusing grasp. "Sissy doesn't steal. And I don't like you manhandling my kid," Mama screamed. "She's been sick."

"Fine. Keep her home then, and you stay home with her. You're fired."

Mama followed the man halfway down the block yelling. "That's fine. Just fine with me. I was going to quit anyway. You can have your lousy job, you old . . . milk toast."

My smug look of satisfaction faded when Mama grabbed me by the shoulder and demanded an answer. Unfortunately, one of the chocolate bars fell from my coat pocket to the floor. Mama went into a fit of rage. She jerked me up and nearly disjointed my arm, pushing me toward the bedroom.

To my delighted relief, Uncle came barging into the bedroom before I'd received three swats.

The next few hours turned into a screaming chaos with Mama, Uncle, and Aunt in a three-way screaming match. My uncle was upset because Mama lost her job, then Aunt got on Mama's side, which sent my uncle further into a tirade. Then, amid tears and apologies to Uncle, Mama sent me and Lil Bub to pack.

My brother and I exchanged a look of victory as we jerked things from the drawers and stuffed them into brown paper bags. My heart pounded toward home. When we pulled out of the drive, I waved at Aunt and Uncle enthusiastically. The last thing I heard was the monotonous plunk of melting snow dripping from the roof.

"How long will it take to get home?" I blurted before we were even out of the yard.

"Sit down and shut up," Mama said as she fumbled with a road map. She began to cry in great torrents, sobbing and wiping all the way into Flagstaff, where she pulled the car over to a filling station and stopped.

"I have to use the phone," Mama said, rummaging through her purse.

"Are you callin Dad?" Lil Bub asked, jumping to his knees. "Are you tellin him we're on our way?"

Mama didn't answer at first. She looked at both of us and took in a deep breath. "We aren't going back to

Oklahoma. I don't know what I'm going to do. I'll call your aunt out in California. Maybe we can go there."

When Mama crawled out to use the phone, Lil Bub began to bawl. "Oh, Sissy, we just have to go home. We have to."

"Don't worry," I said, reaching over the seat and patting his shoulder. "We will."

The words sent a surge of spirit through me, but when Mama returned, it was hard for me to find the courage to start.

"We both want to go home, Mama," I blurted.

"You're too young to understand," Mama said.

"Understand what?" I snapped. "That our feelings don't count? I understand one thing — Shorty's a better parent than you."

Mama turned and slapped me with a deliberate pop. The shock rattled me only for a moment.

"You can hit me, Mama. You can beat me to a pulp, but you can't keep me away from the farm any longer. No matter how far you go, I'm gonna get home to my farm and Shorty. I'll run away and take Lil Bub with me."

"Sissy Gal, shut your mouth," Mama said, clinching her teeth.

Lil Bub sobbed through a cough and crawled over the seat, landing in a lump beside me.

"I'll never leave the farm again, Mama, never," I continued in a half-crazed ramble, my face stinging and my pride unleashed in a burst of stubborn strength. "Home. H-O-M-E. A family's place of residence. The social unit formed by a family living together."

"I wish somehow," Mama started, wiping emotion from her face, "somehow I could make you understand my feelings. I know that you're angry, Sissy, but believe me, I do love you and want what's best for you."

"If you love us, you'll take us home and stay there," I said. "I hate you. I hate you for breakin your promise about leavin with the car, for lyin about the trip just bein a vacation, for draggin us away from home." I spat the words with a hiss. "You don't give a damn how *we* feel. You're just thinkin about your ownself."

Mama reached across the seat, grabbed me with both hands, and shook me in an angry rage that ended in an attempt to hold me. I slid back against the seat like a rag doll, glaring at her.

When she finally started down the highway, I sat, shocked by my outburst and all the things I'd said. The piercing thoughts had been diving and swimming around in my head for months, like starving minnows in a stagnate pool, snatching at anything that moved. They'd nibbled day after miserable day, and I'd held them in silence. I'd thought a lot about all of it. The way I saw it, taking on a family was sort of like a 4-H project. It was a responsibility. If you didn't want it, you didn't take it. But once you did take it, you stood by it, rain or shine. You couldn't just wake up one bright morning and decide to do something else, walk off, and let your sheep starve.

When the afternoon light dimmed to dusk and car lights started reflecting off of the window, Lil Bub leaned toward the boxes on his side and I melted toward the car door.

Mama turned once and pulled a blanket up over our feet. As soon as she turned back to the road, I kicked the blanket to the floor. I thought of her earlier words, "I wish I could make you understand." I squirmed and drummed my foot against the window.

"I'll never understand," I said in a whisper. "Never in ten million, trillion, quadrillion years."

The next morning I awoke with the familiar smothering car sickness. Mama stopped at a small dusty store, went in, and returned with water and two pills. I took them without hesitating, anxious to make the sick feeling disappear.

The remainder of the journey was a blur. I became so sleepy that I couldn't keep my eyes open. Once, late in the afternoon, I sat up when Mama pulled the Studebaker to a stop in front of a roadside cafe. I couldn't stir enough to go but looked around and thought that I recognized the town as one we'd passed through before.

A flash of hope zipped though me, then I wilted back and closed my eyes as the drugged sleep pulled me out of consciousness.

XI

I sat up in the car and rubbed my eyes in disbelief. Life burst into me with a rush of thumping. Tears slid easily down my cheeks. They were tears of complete happiness. We were home.

Leaning forward, I peeked over the seat and could see Mama slumped against the door sleeping. She must have driven in late and decided not to wake everyone. I started to squeal out my joy to Lil Bub, who lay on the seat next to me, but something stopped me. I wanted to be alone on the farm in the springtime morning.

I touched the door handle and it clicked, sounding as loud as a shotgun in my ears. My little brother and mother remained quiet, so I squeaked the door open, slid out, and left it ajar. I crept ever so lightly to the house, looking everywhere for my dog.

Putting my nose against my bedroom window, I could see Sis, twisted into the covers, the pillow over her head. I tiptoed around and peeked on the back porch where Bub slept and was relieved to see the shock of cotton hair against the pillow.

I peeled off my shoes and socks and wiggled my toes into the damp grass, then ran toward the barn calling Shorty. I scurried through the chickens as they pecked in the barnyard, and the hens scattered in a loud, clucking fury, sending feathers drifting to the ground.

"Shorty."

To the garden, across the orchard, beneath the flowering trees, across the creek, faster and faster I ran, my bare feet gently touching soft green, until finally, I fell in a giggling heap beneath my willow tree.

"Shorty, where are you buddy?" I put my face against the damp ground and smelled it, then I kissed the farm, burying my face in its grass, and stretched out long on my tummy, then flipped to my back. "Probably out chasin rabbits this mornin."

The tickling willow branches feathered down across my arms. The familiar feeling lifted my heart with the sweetness of home. I scooted next to my tree and hugged it. "I'll never leave you again," I said. "Never."

I traveled in my mind down the Trail of Tears and thought of the Cherokee people — what a joy they would have had in returning to their homeland.

Shorty's familiar "errf" came from the yard, and I heard squeals and laughter cut through the morning stillness. I jumped and took off in a dead run. My buddy saw me coming and met me halfway, between the granary and the house. He sat down, threw his head back, and howled out a great welcome. I scooped him up and nuzzled him close while he planted sloppy kisses all over my neck, face, and arms.

"I love you," I told him. "And I've missed you somethan awful."

My dog wiggled eagerly out of my arms and dashed in tight circles around me, barking excited "yeps." We romped and rolled in the damp grass until our reunion was complete. Then I carried him toward the yard, where the voices were still sounding.

Dad picked me and my dog up and tossed us into the air, then lifted my chin and looked into my eyes.

"You've grown three inches, P Jink," he said with a wide grin.

Sis stared at me. She had on a wrinkled nightshirt and her long hair hung in curlers, loose and tangled.

"Hi, Sissy." The words came out without a trace of her old teasing and she had a look of genuine happiness to see me. It came to me that Sis and I would one day be good friends. It was a startling thought.

Out of the corner of my eye, I saw Dad take Mama's hand and give her a little hug. Hope flitted through me like a butterfly darting out across clover. The flutter of hope made me angry. It didn't matter to me what Mama did anymore. She could go to Egypt for all I cared. I was never leaving the farm again.

Sis reached and felt one of the long curls that had replaced my ponytails. "I like your hair. You look all grown up."

I gave her a little grin and snuggled Shorty closer to my neck.

"He missed you bad," Sis said. "Sometimes I'd talk to him and give him some extra scraps."

"Thanks," I said, looking around the yard.

"Lil Bub's looking for Shadow. I'm afraid she's . . . gone."

My sister's words made my heart stop. Had Dad hauled Shadow off or shot her? As if Sis was reading my mind, she continued.

"It wasn't Dad. After you two left, she just began to disappear sometimes. The longer you stayed away, the more she left. Finally, she just didn't come home."

For a moment, a deep sadness interfered with the joy of home. I could imagine what I would feel if Shorty hadn't been home to greet me.

"I better find Lil Bub," I said.

"Bub's up at the barn milking. Maybe he's around there."

I heard milk buckets clattering as I passed the chute. I didn't avoid it as usual. I'd even missed the awful branding, castrating, and dehorning of the cattle. Walking quietly into the stall, I paused. Bub sat on the milk stool, his head tight against Mot's flank, his hands busy. The quick streams of milk pounded against the bottom of the bucket. The barn cats purred at Bub's feet, and Bub whistled a snappy tune.

When I walked into the barn, I stood for a few silent moments in shock. My brother's legs were sprawled up and out, and his boots were as big as Dad's. It seemed to me that Dad and Sis hadn't changed at all in nine months, but my older brother had grown into a man. His unruly cotton hair was slicked back neat with oil, and muscles rippled beneath his clean T-shirt.

I took a step toward him and stopped. A chuckle shook me. I picked up a long straw from the barn floor and crept up. Carefully, I touched the back of Bub's neck and ran the straw across his ear.

"Fly, leave me . . ." He spun around, swatting. When he saw me, he jumped and stood towering over me. I leaped toward him and hugged him around the waist. Bub fumbled into the hug.

"Where'd you learn to do that?" he asked.

"Aunt taught me. She was a great hugger. Kind of nice, huh?"

"Yeah," Bub grinned. "Kind of different from our house."

"You've changed," I said.

"Have I?" Bub asked, flexing his arm muscles and drawing back his shoulders. "I've been working out."

For a second I felt uncomfortable. Bub not only looked like a grown man, his voice was different, deep and booming. I felt a sadness come over me. Maybe we won't be good friends anymore, I thought.

"Looky here," he said. I stared in awe as my brother retrieved a blue corduroy FFA jacket with his name, Phillip Jacobs, in gold embroidered letters.

"Can I touch it?" I asked in awe.

Bub got a serious, doubtful look, lifted one shoulder, then let it fall in a shrug. His face slid into the familiar, one-sided grin. "Is a pig's ass pork?" he said, then howled at his own words.

I felt relief spread through me as I ran my fingers across the softness. It was the same old Bub.

Our conversation stopped when a small shadow appeared in the doorway. I looked up and my heart immediately turned sad. Lil Bub stood there, his hands jammed down tight in his overalls pockets.

"My dog gave up on me," he said. "She's up and run off."

The words caused a lump in my throat, but to my surprise, my little brother's eyes were dry. He walked to Bub and stuck out his hand.

Bub jerked him up in his arms. "I think I like Sissy's new style better," he said, laughing. "How goes it little brother?"

"She'll be back. I know down in the deepest part of my ownself she hasn't left me for good."

I glanced at Bub, not knowing what to say. I was afraid to give Lil Bub false hope that would only hurt him worse in the end.

"As a matter of fact," Bub said, "I think I caught a glimpse of her just three days ago."

"Really, Bub? Where was she?" Lil Bub grabbed Bub's hand and clung to it.

"Way over in the far pasture in the blackjack thicket. I was driving the tractor back from the field and just saw something fleeting in the corner of my eye. I stopped and called but didn't see a thing after that."

"Well, she's out there," Lil Bub said with quiet resolve. "And she'll be home when she realizes that I need her." Over the next few weeks, my little brother's solid faith never wavered.

"Breakfast," Dad's voice echoed from the yard. "Come and get it while it's hot."

The mixed chatter at the table was so clattering and confused, it sounded like bees around a busy hive. I was starved. The smell of ham gravy and biscuits filled me with a hunger that I hadn't known for months.

"Hey, hey," Dad said, lifting his hand to silence the mob. "You all sound like a flock of southbound honkers." He grinned, and I warmed to the feeling of home. "If I can have the floor a minute, I have something to tell," Dad said.

Everything quieted. It was unusual for Dad to be in such a festive mood at mealtime.

"Strangest thing," Dad continued, pouring frothy milk from the pitcher into Lil Bub's glass. "Right over in the corner of the wheat field, straight and proud as April, there's a cornstalk."

The words drifted slowly into my ears and struck a nerve. I sucked in my breath and swallowed a wad of honey-soaked biscuit that hung in my throat. Bub pounded me on the back.

After I choked and coughed, finally quieting, Dad continued.

"It's always a puzzle how volunteers come up," he said. "Kind of intrigues me."

My mind reeled. Could it be? The scene from the garden the day I attacked the cornstalk came vividly back to me. I was thankful when the chatter renewed around the table. My face was flushed with guilt.

That evening, I finally had the opportunity. After supper, Shorty and I slipped quietly away and ran down the dirt path. I climbed atop the splintered corner post, pulling my dog into my lap. When I shaded my eyes from the setting sun and stared at the cornstalk, a flood of mixed emotions came floating up in me. There was no doubting it — I'd buried the evidence of my wrath in the exact same spot. It stood, waving in the wind just above the ripening wheat, sticking out like a black chick in a hen house full of white leghorns.

"It's our cornstalk," I said to Shorty in a whispered choke.

Even though no one could ever possibly guess the truth, I burned with guilt. I thought the situation over for a long while, staring at the stalk and hugging my dog. I had an almost irresistible urge to go pull it up and carry it off as far as my feet could trod. But, of course, I couldn't do it. Dad now had an attachment to my old acquaintance.

"It's your cornstalk." Bub's voice came from behind me.

I almost fell face forward off my post. Shorty wiggled out of my arms and jumped to the ground, giving Bub a little "eerrf."

I turned and glared at my brother. "What?" I asked with an innocent tone.

Bub grinned at me. "Come on, Sissy," Bub said, walking off. "Think I'll go down to the grapevines and have a smoke."

I walked behind him in silence, my mind alive with a hundred questions.

Flopping beneath the giant elms near the creek, Bub took out his pocket knife and began carving the thin end of a grapevine. "Try one?" he asked, shoving the finished stump toward me.

I hesitated, weighing the delight of the sin against the severe consequence it could hold. I'd always wanted to give it a try. "Sure," I said, immediately pleased with my adult decision.

For a few moments, the two of us sat, stretched out long in the afternoon sun, backs against the wide elm. Shorty cuddled next to me, his head in my lap, and closed his eyes.

"Yep," Bub finally said. "I saw you attack the cornstalk that day, then bury it in the wheat field."

I stared in disbelief. "Why didn't you say somethan?"

Bub's blue eyes crinkled toward me. "Cause, Sissy, you deserved a temper tantrum. I reckon I decided to let you have it in peace."

"What do you mean, I deserved it?"

"You hold too much inside you, Sissy Gal. You worry too much about things you can't change. It's a big job."

I sucked the smoke down and wiggled my toes into the warm breeze, drinking in the rapture of being on the

farm, with my dog, and having conversation with my
brother. A mild dizziness increased my temporary pleasure of being with Bub, listening to his philosophy.

"Bub, how come you ran off just before we went to
Arizona? Didn't say good-bye?"

"I reckon it was just too hard for me to do."

I listened to the stirring leaves overhead and
watched a beetle struggle with his seed cargo through
the soft dust. "What mostly do you think about, Bub?"

"Mostly girls," Bub said, a hint of mystery in his
voice. "The way they walk and talk and smell."

I turned my eyes on him. For the first time, I noticed
the wisp of blond hair on his upper lip. It startled me.
Bub was getting a mustache. I thought about Carolyn,
who I'd seen a few moments that afternoon. She told
me that some girls in our grade played spin the bottle
with boys out behind the school while I was gone. And I
was shocked when I noticed she was wearing a bra.

Everything was changing, moving ahead, and I
couldn't do anything to stop it. Inhaling the smoke with
a slow draw, I suddenly felt cold and sweaty. I moved
my dog off my lap, knelt against the tree, and puked.

Bub put a large hand on my shoulder. "You okay?"

I was embarrassed and humiliated. I looked away
from him, my face burning.

"Yeah, I reckon."

"It's nothin to be ashamed of, Sissy. Some of my
buddies earped the first time, too."

"Bub," I said, standing, clinging to the tree. I tried to
wet my lips with my tongue, but it was parched and

swollen thicker than a cow's cud. I tossed the grapevine in the creek and watched the disgusting thing get slammed away in the rising current. "Bub, I hate it when things change."

"Yeah," Bub said. "It's scary."

We walked back through the field, and when the cornstalk came back into view, I couldn't quit staring at it.

"I kept your sock money in the cellar, Sissy. I didn't touch a cent of it. What are you gonna do with it?"

Stopping, I stared coldly at the stalk. I thought about all of my useless efforts to figure Mama out, to keep her home. How it all backfired.

"I don't know. I reckon it ain't too important now." The thought of Cootie Brown came into my mind, and I shivered. "Bub, I feel like the cornstalk is whisperin to me, but I can't hear what it's sayin."

"Maybe it's sayin, 'You're stubborn, you're stubborn, you're stubborn," he said, singing out the words. Then he let out a fine roll of booming laughter.

"No, really, Bub. It's like I buried it there and tried to hide it. Now look at it. What do you suppose it means?"

Bub turned and stared at the stiff stalk waving proudly from the wheat field. He looked at it for a long time, then turned without saying anything and started talking again.

"What was it like out in Arizona anyway?"

The question made me turn from the cornstalk and start walking toward the house. I thought of the cocoon of snow wrapping me inside the little cramped house, the big school without my dog, the homesickness that hurt through my skin.

"That bad?" Bub said, touching me on the shoulder.

"Bub, I'm never leavin my dog or this farm again. Never."

He shifted his weight from one foot to the other and let out a sigh. "Sissy, maybe the cornstalk is sayin that things change. I mean, you jerked him up out of the garden and snatched him over there in a strange place, but there he is, straight and proud as ever."

His words made my face turn red. "You aren't the one that got jerked up and taken to Arizona. Lived in a house the size of a shoe box with a pine-needle backyard, went to school with Indians that wouldn't be friendly . . ."

Bub threw his hands in the air. "Sorry, Sissy."

"I'm never leavin this farm again. Mama can't make me."

Bub let out a soft chuckle. "It's me, Sissy. Don't get mad. I'm on your side."

As we walked on in silence, I thought of the Navajo kids at the school in Flagstaff, and a strange yearning stirred within me. I missed them in a way and even loved them — their slow movements and steady, dark eyes. But their rejection of me would always bring back the image of Cootie beneath the school steps and cause a burning in my soul.

XII

The direct connection between my parents' drinking and their fighting became more and more obvious to me that summer. On one particular Saturday afternoon, when they sat in the yard at the picnic table and began to sip homebrew, I got an ominous feeling.

It always started that way. They'd sit, talk, and laugh together in the highest of moods for awhile. But as the day progressed and the drinking continued, the tide would gradually turn. One of them would get angry, an argument would begin, then intensify, and often would carry on late into the night.

So that day, when they were in the early, joyous stages of the ritual, I got an idea. I'd been aching for a chance to spend some of my hard-earned money. After setting aside enough to buy Shorty a genuine leather collar, I decided that an outing to the Nine Mile Corner for hamburgers would be a great treat for us.

Sis had just received her driving permit and leaped at any opportunity to use the car.

I approached the picnic table with hesitation, listening for the tone of my parents' conversation.

"What is it, Sissy?" Dad's voice was not impatient.

"Well, I was wondering. I have my money, you know. I wanted to take Sis and Bub and Lil Bub out for hamburgers at the Nine Mile Corner."

Dad's face slid into a nice smile, and he winked at Mama. Digging into his overalls pocket, he came up with the keys to the pickup and tossed them to me. "Sis can drive you."

An hour later, the four of us sat in a booth at the Nine Mile Corner in a festivity of thick cheeseburgers, golden french fries, and icy Dr. Peppers.

"This is grand, Sissy — thanks," Sis said.

"How gracious," Bub said, "considering part of it is your money."

"Who cares," Sis said, smiling. "That's all past. And, now that I have my driving permit nothing bothers me."

"You still going to Hollywood and marry Elvis? Lois Patricia Presley," Bub teased. "Has a nice ring to it."

"No," Sis said in a tempered tone, blinking her eyes several times to add emphasis. "I've decided that he just isn't right for me."

Bub let out a choke of laughter and fell backward into the booth. "Sis, if I could buy you for what you're worth and sell you for what you think you're worth, I'd be richer than Sissy."

Glancing at Bub's fine FFA jacket, I thought for a moment about my secret dream and how girls weren't allowed to join the Future Farmers of America. With a spurt of excitement, I decided that I would be the first girl to own a grand blue jacket like Bub's.

"What're you gonna do with the rest of yur money, Sissy?" Lil Bub asked, slurping down a gulp of soda pop.

It amazed me that my brother could remain in such good spirits with his dog still gone. But every morning he said, "Shadow will probably be home today." The first two weeks it bothered me, and I was tempted to try to prepare him for the possibility that his dog might not return. But something invisible had stopped me.

"Gonna buy Shorty a grand leather collar with some of it," I said. I let my hand fall to the floor and stroked my friend. Shorty's tail slapped against the booth with loud whacks. "Maybe with little red stones sparkling."

The owner of the Nine Mile Corner, Ida, first said that dogs weren't allowed. But after I explained it was a special occasion and that Shorty had helped earn the money, she relented.

Lil Bub jumped to his knees, eyes sparkling. "Can we get Shadow one, too? Please, Sissy. Wouldn't she be grand?"

"A millionaire like you should be able to afford two dog collars, Sissy." Bub's eyes held mine in a fixed expression.

Sis squinted her eyes into a disapproving worry frown but kept quiet.

"Sure, Lil Bub. Then I'm gonna hang onto the rest of it, just in case . . . we need it or somethan."

As if Sis and Bub read my thoughts, the festive mood at the table seemed to change. A long silence hung, and the dark feeling that had begun that morning when I saw Mama and Dad drinking sifted over me, making me squirm.

"What is it, Sissy?" Bub asked.

"I . . . don't know."

"Well," Sis said, wiping her hands on the paper napkin. "If we leave now, we can drive back the long way, around the section."

When Sis parked the old pickup in the gravel drive, we all sat for a moment in a suspended silence. The assortment of boxes and suitcases that would later become a symbol of my mother's life were strung across the yard in a jagged path.

"Here we go again," Sis said, letting out a long sigh.

"Not me," I choked, hugging my dog. "I'm not goin anywhere."

We were still sitting in the pickup, looking, when Dad came out of the house. Walking toward the shop, he stopped when he saw us all staring in silence. He came to the end of the sidewalk and motioned for us to get out of the truck. Standing rigid in front of him, I clung to my dog.

"Your mother's leaving. Next week we're going over to Pawhuska and file for a divorce." Dad's voice was dry and cold.

The screen door slammed, and Mama came walking out with more of her stuff. Setting the boxes down, she approached.

The hurting tightness clutched immediately at my throat.

"I love all of you, and I'm sorry. But I'd like for any or all of you to come into Ponca and live with . . ."

"I'm stayin," I said before Mama could finish. "I'm never leavin this farm again." Then, not wanting to hear anyone else make their decision, I turned and started off, holding Shorty tight.

Mama worked into the night, packing the Studebaker to the roof with boxes, clothes, and suitcases. Voices rang and fell in a monotonous tone from the yard. I lay numb beneath my willow tree. I didn't allow myself to think about who might be going or staying. When the pain became so tight in my throat that I couldn't breathe, I thought of the cellar — the flickering light against secure, secret walls.

"We can't stop her from leavin," I whispered to my dog, "but she can't make us say good-bye again." I jumped up and took off in a dead run.

In the dim moonlight, it was hard to locate the cellar. I stepped off the distance three times before I finally felt the door beneath the charcoal dirt. Once inside, I had no problem finding the matches and lighting the candles. I sat on the cot hugging Shorty close.

"We're safe now, buddy. No one can hurt us or take us away from each other. Maybe we'll just spend our time hidden here in the cellar and live like renegade Apaches, runnin from the white soldiers."

Shorty squeezed out of my grasp and walked to the steps. He looked longingly up to the door and whined. He never had liked it that well in the cellar. I sometimes had to push and shove to get him down the steps. I tried to ignore his pleading, but he turned his whine into a shrill howl that echoed against the cool walls.

I put my fingers in my ears. "You can howl all night, buddy, but I'm not lettin you out of my sight."

When the door above cracked open and the gray shadow cast down over me, my heart stopped.

"Sissy," Bub's voice boomed out of the darkness. He stepped down, reached, and jerked me into his strong arms.

"Oh, Bub," I rattled, "Mama's leavin for good this time, I know it. What if the county comes for us and we all end up like Cootie Brown and get put in foster homes and get separated and . . ."

Bub shook me gently, and the tears that flooded my face scattered like rain. "Sissy, Sissy," he said, putting a calloused hand on my hair. "The things you put in that head of yours." Then he stepped back, wiped his face with his sleeve, and bent to blow out the candles.

Just before the lights flickered out, I saw the dampness on my brother's cheeks. The sight made my shoulders tremble. When Bub touched me to guide me out of the darkness, he felt the trembling. He took off his FFA jacket and draped it over my shoulders.

"Sissy, you know Dad. Do you think he'd ever let us get separated — let us live like the Brown kids? Lay down his responsibility like that?"

His words made all of my fears seem foolish. I thought about my rigid, hard-working father. Bub was right. Dad wouldn't let that happen. Why had the worry haunted me so?

My brother gently pushed me toward the steps. "Come on, Sissy, you have to say good-bye to Mama. Dad sent me to find you."

I balked and set my feet stubbornly. "I'm not goin. She can leave if she wants, but I'm not sayin good-bye."

Bub pushed me along up and out into the moonlight. "I know it's hard," Bub said. "Come on, at least let her tell *you* good-bye."

We started single file across the field in the moonlight.
"I'm not movin into Ponca City. Sounds like Sis may move into Ponca later, but Lil Bub wants to stay. Mama's pretty torn up about it."

I didn't want to hear it — any of it. I put my hands over my ears.

The moon broke out big and round from the shifting clouds and a nighthawk swooped down after a scampering field mouse. I stopped when I saw the lone cornstalk looming above the wheat, a stiff shadow in the moonlit field.

My hands dropped from my ears. The grim reminder brought the full impact of my futile struggle. "I'm not tellin her good-bye. I don't want to see her again. Ever."

Bub turned and saw me staring at the cornstalk.

"Sissy, you just have to face the fear. Just face it." He took a long step backward and pushed me. I walked three steps and stopped. Bub shook his head in disbe-lief. "You're bullheaded, Sissy," he said. "Dad sent me to fetch you, and you're comin with me if I have to hog tie and carry you."

Finally, after several more quick shoves, I walked on. When we reached the yard, I stopped by the gate. "Come on, Sissy, you have to say good-bye." Bub gave me another quick push.

"I . . . I'll be beneath my willow tree," I said and bounded off so that he couldn't drag me into the house.

When the car lights moved out from the house and started toward the road, I felt the pain in my belly tighten. Mama pulled the Studebaker to a stop and walked down to the willow tree. I turned my back and stared blindly into the trunk of my tree, holding Shorty with a death grip.

"Sissy Gal, I'm leavin now." Mama's voice shook with emotion.

"You'll be sorry," I said, my voice as sharp and cold as an icicle. "Sorry for breakin up our family."

After a long hesitation she said, "Sissy Gal, I love you and don't you forget it. You're angry and that's all right." Her voice jerked with a sob, then she reached and ran a gentle hand over my curly hair. "Good-bye, Sissy Gal."

When the car lights disappeared down the gravel road, I turned. My throat hurt every time I breathed, like it would explode if I didn't cry. But the tears hung inside me like a fishhook stuck deep into the gut of a fish, burning and choking me with pain.

Darkness filtered down over the creek. An owl started hooting nearby, and a coyote yelped from a distant hill. I heard something and looked to see Lil Bub, walking up, dragging Bub's army blanket, with Dad following.

"Your brother wants to sleep outside with you," Dad said. He kneeled down and worked a willow limb between thick fingers. "Everything will be okay, P Jink," he said. "Don't worry, we'll get leveled out." The words came with great effort, and when he paused, it seemed like he wanted to say more but couldn't.

From out of the darkness, I heard a familiar whine, and Shorty squeezed from my grasp. Then Lil Bub squealed out a cry, crawling off into the darkness. When I first caught sight of the pointed head and shimmering coat, I blinked in disbelief.

"I'll be damned," Dad mumbled. "She's come back."

Shadow scooted up close to her young master and whined out her feelings while Shorty licked her under the chin, his tail flipping over his back.

Dad stood, hesitated a few more minutes, then walked away. My little brother spread the blanket on the ground and pulled Shadow up close to him. I moved on the other side of him, and Shorty scrunched between us.

"What's divorce mean, Sissy?" The question dislodged the tears from inside my brother, and a little sob brought Shadow closer to his neck.

I had to swallow three times to get the words past my throat. "It's . . . it's the end of a marriage."

"The end?" Lil Bub's words cut deep into me, slowly pulling the barbed hook out of my gut, releasing the tears. "Fore long, Sissy, you and me and Shadow and Shorty will be goin up across them terraces to school."

I jerked him close and bit my lip. "That's right, Lil Bub." Then I pulled the blanket up around his feet and reached out to stroke Shadow's long nose. "Glad you're home, girl."

When my little brother's breathing finally settled into a rattling hum, I covered him with the blanket and slid away. Shorty gave Shadow a lick and a whine, then followed me.

My feet went slowly, with soft, determined steps toward the cornstalk. When I caught the first glimpse of the looming stalk in the shadowed moonlight, tears blinded me.

"I hate you," I screamed, standing in front of the stalk and giving it a soft push. It bounced back easily toward me, and I smacked it with a determined punch. "I hate you, I hate you, I hate you!" Squealing like a banshee, I swatted and the stalk bounced until I exhausted myself.

I walked to the creek and searched until I found some ripe pokeberries. Smearing my cheeks and forehead with lines of the purple juice, I knelt and streaked my dog's face. Discarding my shirt, I raised my hands to the night spirits and cried out my anguish, then I returned to the stalk.

Standing straight and silent, I faced my fears. Mama was gone for good, and I knew it in the deepest part of my ownself. Home, as I had known it, would never be the same. For hours, I stood, staring at the looming stalk, letting a storm of violent emotions come and pass until a calm finally sifted over me.

Epilogue

For the next thirty years, the cornstalk haunted me at night. A dream might begin with any circumstance or scene, but the moment I caught a glimpse of the cornstalk, terror would settle upon me. Brutal would often be in the background, laughing and chasing as I fell from cliffs, walked among the dead bodies of my family, or watched my animals suffer.

Throughout every crisis in my life, the cornstalk and Brutal were with me. I studied the meaning of dreams and learned that the nightmares had to do with fear and the loss of security, but knowing that didn't take away the horror. The cornstalk remained my nighttime nemesis.

Thirty-some years after we moved from the farm, I returned to Osage County for a reunion at Braden School. The red brick building, windows boarded up, stood proudly on the hill, now serving as the community center.

Before people arrived, I walked the school grounds, remembering. In the far corner, down in the little valley toward the small white house, I pictured myself with Pat Dog chewing gum on the old porch steps.

"The itsy bitsy spider went up the water sprout." I sang the words in my mind. Then I thought of Shorty and his reassuring nudge against my neck.

Over the years, Shadow and Shorty produced three litters of eight pups. Could there be a half-coyote descendant of Shorty still roaming wild and free in the hills?

The afternoon of the reunion, Miss Alma Hedberg, at ninety-two, posed with me in front of the school steps for pictures. As the photographer prepared his camera, my old teacher extended a frail finger downward.

In front of us, on the sidewalk, were two sets of paw prints.

"Look," I heard my younger brother say, "that has to be Shadow's prints. Wow, Sissy." My brother was on his knees. "These smaller ones must be Shorty's."

A flash of memory hurled me back.

Dad was bent over the school sidewalk making wide sweeps with his trowel, working the soup into solid smoothness. I knelt nearby, shirtless, and pushed a dangling feather from my painted face. I smelled the newness of concrete and the sweetness of spring on the warm wind. Shadow and Shorty appeared at the edge of the school yard, crouched in the deep grass.

"Come," I hollered in an Indian, guttural command. They bolted toward me, sauntering across Dad's sparkling sidewalk, mucking their tracks through the smoothness. "Look, Dad, they left part of themselves behind."

"GET!" Dad bellowed, sending the dogs scurrying back toward the farm. "Damn it all to hell, Sissy, now I have to redo it."

"Don't Dad, pleasseee. What fun to have our dogs in the sidewalk."

Dad looked at me with a perplexed expression. Then he glanced at his watch. "Damn, it's 2:00. I have fifteen minutes to clean up my tools and pack a lunch for work."

"Sissy." It was my brother and sister beside me. "You okay?"

I nodded, numbly, my mind traveling forward to 1982 when my father died beneath his tractor. Somewhere on the wind, I heard the jingle of iced tea from a mason jar and a kildeer give his warning cry.

"Sissy." Lil Bub's voice was laced with concern. "What is it?"

"It's all connected," I mumbled, reaching for Miss Hedberg's hand.

"Yes." My old teacher squeezed my fingers. "It's all connected. When you live as long as I have, Sissy, you don't believe in coincidence."

Sleeping that night in my sister's house near Ponca City, I had a dream. I was on the farm near the creek beneath my willow tree, studying a maze of paw prints, when I heard a familiar "eerf."

In the far distance, I heard Shorty's bark again, "eerf, eerf." Then, in the clear blue of the horizon, I caught a glimpse of a purple speck.

It was Fob, flying toward me, carrying Shorty. When he floated to the ground in front of me, Fob lowered himself and offered his back. I bowed to him in great reverence. Shorty bounced around me, then dived into my arms and nuzzled my neck as I seated myself.

Together, we flew over the farm, and my ears bubbled with the joy of home — Dad's tractor plowing, Mama's voice singing from the kitchen window, Bub's echoing laughter, and Sis's record player with Elvis singing, "Are You Lonesome Tonight?"

Then I spotted the cornstalk still looming in the wheat field and sucked in a gulp of air, but then the fear was gone. "I love you," I shouted. The words burst out of me. Shorty nuzzled my neck, and Fob's feathers tickled my legs. Higher and higher we flew into the clouds. "I love you, I love you."

We were surrounded by a flock of Canadian geese that echoed my words. "I love you, I love you, I love you."

When I stared at the birds, I saw, Mama, Dad, Sis, Bub, Lil Bub, Grandma Carrie, Uncle, and Aunt.

We flew from bright sunshine into night. I looked above but instead of stars, sparkling paw prints scattered across the black sky.

I awoke in my sister's farmhouse, snuggled beneath warm quilts still whispering, "I love you."

For a long time, I lay in the darkness drinking in the

rapture of the dream, taking in each wonderful moment and reliving it in my mind. For the first time since childhood, Fob had returned to me.

In the deepest part of my "ownself" I began to understand. The paw prints were evidence of a journey that began on the old porch steps with a Sears catalog turned upside down. A struggle that led from Shorty and Shadow through my adult years, then back to Braden School. A canine circle of love, a divine sense of security. Paw prints in my soul.